The Singing Word

168 YEARS OF POETRY FROM *The Atlantic*

WALT HUNTER

zando
NEW YORK

Page 194 is a continuation of this copyright page.

zandoprojects.com

First Edition: September 2025

Text design by Neuwirth & Associates, Inc.
Cover design by Paul Spella
Cover art: Painting by Lucy Murray Willis

Library of Congress Control Number: 2025940593

978-1-63893-298-7 (hardcover)
978-1-63893-299-4 (ebook)

10 9 8 7 6 5 4 3 2 1
Manufactured in the United States of America
LKS

For Julian Henry Turner Hunter

CONTENTS

II.
NATURAL LINES

III.
PERSONAL MYTHOLOGIES

FOREWORD

BY *Joshua Bennett*

When I consider the contributions of this new anthology, *The Singing Word*, two literary giants come to mind. The first, featured in these very pages, is Robert Frost. In 1960, during an interview with *The Paris Review*, he said the following:

> I look at a poem as a performance. I look on the poet as a man of prowess, just like an athlete. He's a performer [. . .] The whole thing is performance and prowess and feats of association. Why don't critics talk about those things—what a feat it was to turn that that way, and what a feat it was to remember that, to be reminded of that, by this? Why don't they talk about that? Scoring. You've got to *score*. They say not, but you've got to score, in all the realms—theology, politics, astronomy, history, and the country life around you.

Against and alongside the grain of Frost's offering, I want to linger with his use of the critical term *scoring*. In a triple sense: The poem as a kind of athletic achievement, as mark-making in service of holding one's place in space and time (more on this in a moment), and as an act of musical arrangement. Poems as the way we orchestrate the sounds of everyday occurrence, or else transmute our highest joys, our deepest grief, into alternate forms. Sign and song. Human language distilled to its elemental energies.

This is one way to understand the charismatic framing *The Atlantic* has given us for this new book, this gathering place for the poems that have graced its pages for almost two centuries. That is, as the soaring score of the magazine's work in the world of print: the ever-present music accompanying the photographs and journalistic prose, "the marrow of wit," the soul of this ever-unfolding text. Herein, you will find war songs, love songs, elegies, and odes; you will hear, in a striking range of textures and tones, the history of the United States of America rendered in verse. What's more, the band that Walt Hunter has assembled here is marked by both its charisma and its conflicts—harmonic dissidence rather than univocality or singular purpose. There are poems that read like time capsules, preserving a historical moment, in all its strangeness, for modern eyes. And others that are almost heartbreaking in their prescience, such as Stephen Vincent Benét's "Litany for Dictatorships" ("We thought the light would increase. / Now the long train stands derailed and the bandits loot it").

It's all here, rendered with real, polychromatic complexity, seen through a moving lens magnifying the landscape of our national past. These poems swing, ever elegantly, between recreation, casual observation, and reckoning with the state of the world. They feature baseball, cormorants, wartime, cygnets, the threat of species extinction, old-time religion, Frederick Douglass (more than once), the state of Vermont (also more than once), mountains, physicians, monarch butterflies, the Hudson River. Phil Levine sings to the children of truckers and spark-plug-factory workers in Flint, Michigan, and promises to pass down a gift: a poem of joyful overcoming in the town they now call home, as he once did. James Tate grieves his father, a pilot, whom he sees soaring above him each day, as well as in the bodies of the loved ones he left on Earth. Nikki Giovanni praises her grandparents and the life they made together in coal-country Tennessee, sharing family stories and the light of each other's company. She reminds us of the beauty of her true inheritance, which was not property, she writes, but wisdom, and a more gentle way of being alongside all living things. Mona Van Duyn solos beautifully, offering insight into a lifelong marriage anchored by adoration, telling us what it required, what it fortifies in her world even still. Taken together, these particular poets and poems, among many others in this anthology, brought me back again and again to a kind of refrain: We are lost without one another.

The second figure who has been on my mind as I reflect on the great gift of this anthology, and the set of resources it grants us in the here and now, is none other than the political visionary and polymath par excellence June Jordan. Thirty-four years after Frost's statement about the relationship between poetry and performance, Jordan described her vision for a collective pedagogical project, a community writing program called Poetry for the People, in a *Bookworm* interview: "I don't live in an entirely African American world, a black-and-white world. I try to put together as catholic a syllabus as possible." Within the scope of Jordan's initiative, which she founded in Berkeley, California, in 1986 (and modeled off her transformative late-1960s literary arts program in New York City, the Voice of the Children), students would move each week through the respective poetic traditions of US writers from various racial and ethnic backgrounds, one by one, with the aim of grasping, and ultimately inhabiting, a truly kaleidoscopic sense of a national canon. Students in P4P were also actively trained to teach the course themselves over time. In this way, the class was meant to function as a form of collective inheritance: a method, and a mode of relation, to pass on to the future.

This book is a kind of universal syllabus. Take it into your classrooms, your homes, and afternoons outside under the open sky. It lights a way forward for those of us still devoted to the idea that poetry's ancient work is never over: as a vehicle for consciousness, a bridge between worlds, and a reminder of all we have seen, and survived, together.

INTRODUCTION

BY *Walt Hunter*

Two days after my son was born in early 2024, I began reading every poem *The Atlantic* had printed since the magazine's first issue in November 1857. I wasn't thinking about an anthology, not yet. But I did feel an obligation—and a desire—as the poetry editor to keep one foot firmly in the past. For me, being something of a completist, that meant reading all the poems we had published. Outside, deep January had arrived in Cleveland, Ohio. It felt like the sun hadn't come out for nineteen days. I was awake from 3:30 AM to 10 AM with the baby for the indefinite future. There would never be a better time to do this.

I plunged into the archives, into Ralph Waldo Emerson, Henry Wadsworth Longfellow, and John Greenleaf Whittier, and their successors in the years leading up to the Civil War. I leafed issue by issue, and read the poems within them. Occasionally poems even appeared as the first piece in an issue, among them Julia Ward Howe's "Battle Hymn of the Republic" in February 1862. I read as many as I could out loud while the baby slept, woke, ate, and slept again. Murder ballads, ceremonial odes, pastorals, melodramas—the variety was astonishing. That January was the cloudiest in several decades, but I remember it as full of bright light and constant babble, the first words my child would hear, the poems in this book you're holding.

The history of *Atlantic* poetry has genuine hits (Longfellow's "Paul Revere's Ride," Robert Frost's "Birches") and lost B-sides (Dorothy Leonard's "Beauty Is Gathered like the Rain on Hills"); Nobel laureates (Louise Glück, Rabindranath Tagore) and poet laureates (Billy Collins, Natasha Trethewey, Ada Limón). As I read, I kept track of patterns: a late 1850s obsession with poems about ice skaters, a quatrain craze starting in the 1880s. So many ghost poems, verse about lobstermen, stanzas about fires in Chicago and Boston, forays into nature in California, buoyant verses marking the passage of seasons, tragic tributes to babies who died.

But after three weeks, I was not much closer to the twentieth century. At some point, my child would be walking and, in the pages of the magazine at least, Longfellow would still be very much alive. I had over a hundred years left, and thousands of poems. I tried not to panic; after all, I'd set myself up for this. I cleaned the bottles, turned to the next issue.

Over time, single poems blurred into a larger picture, a kind of giant poem. The chorus of a country swelled through the everyday anthems of ordinary lives; a map came together from the descriptions of American landscapes; a national mythology grew from personal memories and private lives. Moments of individual struggle and success illuminated a country's frustrations, griefs, and joys. Walt Whitman, who published two poems in the magazine, once wrote that "the United States themselves are the greatest poem." I started thinking about an anthology that would tell a story about American poetry, and about the United States, through the poetry of the *Atlantic*.

The nature of "*Atlantic* poetry" has changed dramatically since the mid-nineteenth century. We have yet to publish another fifteen-page narrative poem like James Russell Lowell's "The Cathedral." Nor do we take iambic pentameter for granted anymore. But the *Atlantic*'s faith in its broad audience—diverse, curious, skeptical, intelligent, engaged—has not changed. As I thought about an anthology, I never had in view a doorstopper monument or a coffee-table adornment. I imagined a book that you might read on the bus or subway, carry with you easily, flip through in idle moments. I wanted it to evoke the anthologies I loved best as a child and as an adult—to jolt readers with unexpected discoveries. I was eager to share the bracing experience of turning from Robert Hayden's praise of Frederick Douglass to Robert Lowell's outrage at the unfinished project of emancipation. Or the delight of flipping from a summer mountain as seen by Wallace Stevens to the wintry landscape of Sylvia Plath's imagination. One portfolio of poems might contain mockingbirds, lichens, a dooryard flower or a cormorant. *Atlantic* poems insist on juxtaposing variety and sameness, the prickling of sensation and the dullness of habit.

I decided to move chronologically because I kept hearing echoes across time, ongoing conversations among poets. Each section of the anthology opens with verse published in the first several issues of the magazine—and closes with poems that come right up to the present moment. I found as I was looking through them that the poems fell into three categories: poems that captured American history by turning it into song; poems that charted the sweep of the country, sometimes in the space of a few lines; and poems that chronicled democracy on an intimate, human scale. These thematic lines, there at the founding of the magazine, helped to guide me through the rest of the book. Within those sections, my criterion for inclusion wasn't technical or academic.

The language in the poem had to do something singular and unusual. To put it another way, I wanted to avoid derivative work, poems that risked ringing in too familiar a register. I wanted every poem to feel indispensable, that slippery word. I went by something I can only call feel, picking poems that I hoped a reader would revisit multiple times, whether for the sentiment, the story, the music, or all of the above.

Especially during the first few decades, through the 1880s, the magazine's poems gravitated to stories about vivid characters and events. I've ended up including a number of poems addressed to famous figures, role models for poet and reader alike. Paul Laurence Dunbar honors the memory of Robert Gould Shaw, who led the all-Black 54th Massachusetts Infantry Regiment. Conrad Aiken mourns his late friend, the British poet Rupert Brooke, dead in World War I. Robert Hayden writes in tribute to Frederick Douglass. Lauren K. Alleyne imagines Martin Luther King Jr. writing to Trayvon Martin. These figures have one thing in common. Confronted with hostility to American ideals and the perversion of its institutions, they spoke, wrote, and fought for the freedom promised in its founding.

Yet a similar number of poems commemorate ordinary acts of heroism and the strength of communities. An old woman in Whittier's "Barbara Frietchie" hoists the Union flag as Confederate soldiers pass. A father and child, in Jeannette Nichols's "One Day," have a moment of sudden clarity and connection on a beautiful Vermont morning. You'll find the children of Flint, Michigan in these pages, and a high school football coach, and suburban couples tossing anxiously in their beds. James Russell Lowell's daughter, Natasha Trethewey's mother, James Tate's father, Nikki Giovanni's grandparents—as I looked for poems that moved me, I found American families, tested in the crucible of circumstance and tragedy.

Atlantic poems have represented the country's wildly divergent visions of a good life—and railed against thwarted hopes for it. This is not to say that *Atlantic* poetry has focused narrowly on the country, but that it has deepened our understanding of what the country is. These poems rebut the parochialism and tribalism that dog our present, even as they appeal to universal experiences and values, rendered in startling detail through the stories of particular lives. If that makes them sound a little like good journalism, that's where the book starts, in a way: with "Paul Revere's Ride," and its urgent exhortation to *listen*.

What emerged as I read was an optimism and realism—a sense that, however bad things are, the idea of America is worth fighting for, and worth questioning and scrutinizing in new ways. The poems here are not ancillary ornaments, but rather essential vehicles for that search. Their energy and their explosive charge come from their devotion to the truth: the hope for American improvement is indelibly wedded to the critique, sometimes blistering, sometimes mournful, of the status quo.

And yet, as Richard Hugo reminds us in "A Good View from Flagstaff"—my favorite, I confess, of all the poems in this book—"let's take it as it is":

> A good view here. We ignore the mean acts
> in the houses though we can't forget they go on

daily with the soul's attrition. We are certain
why the plow horse limps. Spread the way it is
by wind, the world in cultivated patchwork
claims we travel on the right freight one day
and the years are gone. At worst
they're more than nothing. The best friends
we remember took us home the way we are.

Hugo starts and ends his poem in the grubby, unheroic ordinary, the daily upkeep of individual moral courage and resilience. These poems don't just showcase values we hope are American. They give those values meaning by setting them loose in vivid, memorable language.

The belief in the future isn't the property of any one faction or political party; it's a feature of poetry itself, which tries to express in words what hasn't yet appeared in life. In its pursuit of the American idea, *The Atlantic* has published and preserved much of the greatest modern poetry we have.

Poetry, no matter how whimsical, oblique, or difficult, is rarely, if ever, an evasion of the times in which we live. Poems solicit the human compulsion to recite words out loud, memorize lines and passages, appreciate the complexities of others and emphasize with them. Poems arrive in the middle of political and personal doldrums, torpor, inertia, ignorance, complacency, even despair. They're like the spark that flies from Revere's horse-hooves as he rides: *Atlantic* poems produce that flicker–flinty, bright, and unpredictable, "in the hour of darkness and peril and need." They quicken the words we use every day. However briefly, desperately, and courageously, they make our words sing.

I.

NATIONAL ANTHEMS

Paul Revere's Ride

BY *Henry Wadsworth Longfellow*

Listen, my children, and you shall hear
Of the midnight ride of Paul Revere,
On the eighteenth of April, in Seventy-Five:
Hardly a man is now alive
Who remembers that famous day and year.

He said to his friend,—"If the British march
By land or sea from the town to-night,
Hang a lantern aloft in the belfry-arch
Of the North-Church-tower, as a signal-light,—
One if by land, and two if by sea;
And I on the opposite shore will be,
Ready to ride and spread the alarm
Through every Middlesex village and farm,
For the country-folk to be up and to arm."

Then he said good-night, and with muffled oar
Silently rowed to the Charlestown shore,
Just as the moon rose over the bay,
Where swinging wide at her moorings lay
The Somerset, British man-of-war:
A phantom ship, with each mast and spar

Across the moon, like a prison-bar,
And a huge, black hulk, that was magnified
By its own reflection in the tide.

Meanwhile, his friend, through alley and street
Wanders and watches with eager ears,
Till in the silence around him he hears
The muster of men at the barrack-door,
The sound of arms, and the tramp of feet,
And the measured tread of the grenadiers
Marching down to their boats on the shore.

Then he climbed to the tower of the church,
Up the wooden stairs, with stealthy tread,
To the belfry-chamber overhead,
And startled the pigeons from their perch
On the sombre rafters, that round him made
Masses and moving shapes of shade,—
Up the light ladder, slender and tall,
To the highest window in the wall,
Where he paused to listen and look down
A moment on the roofs of the town,
And the moonlight flowing over all.

Beneath, in the churchyard, lay the dead
In their night-encampment on the hill,
Wrapped in silence so deep and still,

That he could hear, like a sentinel's tread,
The watchful night-wind, as it went
Creeping along from tent to tent,
And seeming to whisper, "All is well!"
A moment only he feels the spell
Of the place and the hour, the secret dread
Of the lonely belfry and the dead;
For suddenly all his thoughts are bent
On a shadowy something far away,
Where the river widens to meet the bay,—
A line of black, that bends and floats
On the rising tide, like a bridge of boats.

Meanwhile, impatient to mount and ride,
Booted and spurred, with a heavy stride,
On the opposite shore walked Paul Revere
Now he patted his horse's side,
Now gazed on the landscape far and near,
Then impetuous stamped the earth,
And turned and tightened his saddle-girth;
But mostly he watched with eager search
The belfry-tower of the old North Church,
As it rose above the graves on the hill,
Lonely, and spectral, and sombre, and still.

And lo! as he looks, on the belfry's height,
A glimmer, and then a gleam of light!

He springs to the saddle, the bridle he turns,
But lingers and gazes, till full on his sight
A second lamp in the belfry burns!

A hurry of hoofs in a village-street,
A shape in the moonlight, a bulk in the dark,
And beneath from the pebbles, in passing, a spark
Struck out by a steed that flies fearless and fleet:
That was all! And yet, through the gloom and the light,
The fate of a nation was riding that night;
And the spark struck out by that steed, in his flight,
Kindled the land into flame with its heat.

It was twelve by the village-clock,
When he crossed the bridge into Medford town.
He heard the crowing of the cock,
And the barking of the farmer's dog,
And felt the damp of the river-fog,
That rises when the sun goes down.

It was one by the village-clock,
When he rode into Lexington.
He saw the gilded weathercock
Swim in the moonlight as he passed,
And the meeting-house windows, blank and bare,
Gaze at him with a spectral glare,

As if they already stood aghast
At the bloody work they would look upon.

It was two by the village-clock,
When he came to the bridge in Concord town.
He heard the bleating of the flock,
And the twitter of birds among the trees,
And felt the breath of the morning-breeze
Blowing over the meadows brown.
And one was safe and asleep in his bed
Who at the bridge would be first to fall,
Who that day would be lying dead,
Pierced by a British musket-ball.

You know the rest. In the books you have read
How the British regulars fired and fled,—
How the farmers gave them ball for ball,
From behind each fence and farmyard-wall,
Chasing the red-coats down the lane,
Then crossing the fields to emerge again
Under the trees at the turn of the road,
And only pausing to fire and load.

So through the night rode Paul Revere;
And so through the night went his cry of alarm
To every Middlesex village and farm,—

A cry of defiance, and not of fear,—
A voice in the darkness, a knock at the door,
And a word that shall echo forevermore!
For, borne on the night-wind of the Past,
Through all our history, to the last,
In the hour of darkness and peril and need,
The people will waken and listen to hear
The hurrying hoof-beat of that steed,
And the midnight-message of Paul Revere.

Dirge

FOR ONE WHO FELL IN BATTLE

BY *Thomas William Parsons*

Room for a Soldier! lay him in the clover;
He loved the fields, and they shall be his cover;
Make his mound with hers who called him once her lover:
Where the rain may rain upon it,
Where the sun may shine upon it,
Where the lamb hath lain upon it,
And the bee will dine upon it.

Bear him to no dismal tomb under city churches;
Take him to the fragrant fields, by the silver birches,
Where the whippoorwill shall mourn, where the oriole perches:
Make his mound with sunshine on it,
Where the bee will dine upon it,
Where the lamb hath lain upon it,
And the rain will rain upon it.

Busy as the busy bee, his rest should be the clover;
Gentle as the lamb was he, and the fern should be his cover;
Fern and rosemary shall grow my soldier's pillow over:
Where the rain may rain upon it,
Where the sun may shine upon it,

Where the lamb hath lain upon it,
And the bee will dine upon it.

Sunshine in his heart, the rain would come full often
Out of those tender eyes which evermore did soften;
He never could look cold, till we saw him in his coffin.
Make his mound with sunshine on it,
Where the wind may sigh upon it,
Where the moon may stream upon it,
And Memory shall dream upon it.

"Captain or Colonel,"—whatever invocation
Suit our hymn the best, no matter for thy station,—
On thy grave the rain shall fall from the eyes of a mighty nation!
Long as the sun doth shine upon it
Shall grow the goodly pine upon it,
Long as the stars do gleam upon it
Shall Memory come to dream upon it.

Battle Hymn of the Republic

BY *Julia Ward Howe*

Mine eyes have seen the glory of the coming of the Lord:
He is trampling out the vintage where the grapes of wrath are stored;
He hath loosed the fateful lightning of His terrible swift sword:
His truth is marching on.

I have seen Him in the watch-fires of a hundred circling camps,
They have builded Him an altar in the evening dews and damps;
I can read His righteous sentence by the dim and flaring lamps:
His day is marching on.

I have read a fiery gospel writ in burnished rows of steel:
"As ye deal with my contemners, so with you my grace shall deal;
Let the Hero, born of woman, crush the serpent with his heel,
Since God is marching on."

He has sounded forth the trumpet that shall never call retreat;
He is sifting out the hearts of men before His judgment-seat:
Oh, be swift, my soul, to answer Him! be jubilant, my feet!
Our God is marching on.

In the beauty of the lilies Christ was born across the sea,
With a glory in his bosom that transfigures you and me:
As he died to make men holy, let us die to make men free,
While God is marching on.

Barbara Frietchie

BY *John Greenleaf Whittier*

Up from the meadows rich with corn,
Clear in the cool September morn,

The clustered spires of Frederick stand
Green-walled by the hills of Maryland.

Round about them orchards sweep,
Apple- and peach-tree fruited deep,

Fair as a garden of the Lord
To the eyes of the famished rebel horde,

On that pleasant morn of the early fall
When Lee marched over the mountain-wall,—

Over the mountains winding down,
Horse and foot, into Frederick town.

Forty flags with their silver stars,
Forty flags with their crimson bars,

Flapped in the morning wind: the sun
Of noon looked down, and saw not one.

Up rose old Barbara Frietchie then,
Bowed with her fourscore years and ten;

Bravest of all in Frederick town,
She took up the flag the men hauled down;

In her attic-window the staff she set,
To show that one heart was loyal yet.

Up the street came the rebel tread,
Stonewall Jackson riding ahead.

Under his slouched hat left and right
He glanced: the old flag met his sight.

"Halt!"—the dust-brown ranks stood fast.
"Fire!"—out blazed the rifle-blast.

It shivered the window, pane and sash;
It rent the banner with seam and gash.

Quick, as it fell, from the broken staff
Dame Barbara snatched the silken scarf;

She leaned far out on the window-sill,
And shook it forth with a royal will.

"Shoot, if you must, this old gray head,
But spare your country's flag," she said.

A shade of sadness, a blush of shame,
Over the face of the leader came;

The nobler nature within him stirred
To life at that woman's deed and word:

"Who touches a hair of yon gray head
Dies like a dog! March on!" he said.

All day long through Frederick street
Sounded the tread of marching feet:

All day long that free flag tossed
Over the heads of the rebel host.

Ever its torn folds rose and fell
On the loyal winds that loved it well;

And through the hill-gaps sunset light
Shone over it with a warm good-night.

Barbara Frietchie's work is o'er,
And the Rebel rides on his raids no more.

Honor to her! and let a tear
Fall, for her sake, on Stonewall's bier.

Over Barbara Frietchie's grave
Flag of Freedom and Union, wave!

Peace and order and beauty draw
Round thy symbol of light and law;

And ever the stars above look down
On thy stars below in Frederick town!

Road-Hymn for the Start

BY *William Vaughn Moody*

Leave the early bells at chime,
Leave the kindled hearth to blaze,
Leave the trellised panes where children linger out the waking-time,
Leave the forms of sons and fathers trudging through the misty ways,
Leave the sounds of mothers taking up their sweet laborious days.

Pass them by! even while our soul
Yearns to them with keen distress.
Unto them a part is given; we will strive to see the whole;
Dear shall be the banquet table where their singing spirits press,
Dearer be our sacred hunger and our pilgrim loneliness.

We have felt the ancient swaying
Of the earth before the sun,
On the darkened marge of midnight heard sidereal rivers playing;
Rash it was to bathe our souls there, but we plunged and all was done:
That is lives and lives behind us, and our journey is begun!

Careless where our face is set
Let us take the open way:
What we are no tongue hath told us. Errand-goers who forget?

Soldiers heedless of their harry? Pilgrim people gone astray?
We have heard a voice cry, "Wander!" That was all we heard it say.

Ask no more: 'tis much! 'tis much!
Down the road the day-star calls;
Touched with change in the wide heavens, like a leaf the frost doth touch,
Flames the failing moon a moment ere it shrivels white and falls;
Hid aloft a shy throat holdeth sweet and sweeter intervals.

Leave him still to ease in song
Half his little heart's unrest;
Speech is his, but we may journey toward the life for which we long.
God who gives the bird its anguish maketh nothing manifest,
But upon our lifted foreheads pours the boon of endless quest.

Robert Gould Shaw

BY *Paul Laurence Dunbar*

Why was it that the thunder voice of Fate
Should call thee, studious, from the classic groves,
Where calm-eyed Pallas with still footstep roves,
And charge thee seek the turmoil of the state?
What bade thee hear the voice and rise elate,
Leave home and kindred and thy spicy loaves
To lead th' unlettered and despisèd droves
To manhood's home and thunder at the gate?

Far better the slow blaze of Learning's light,
The cool and quiet of her dearer fane,
Than this hot terror of a hopeless fight,
This bold endurance of the final pain;
Since thou and those who with thee died for right
Have died, the Present teaches, but in vain!

Rupert Brooke

(DIED AT THE DARDANELLES, APRIL 1915)

BY *Conrad Aiken*

You need no praise, nor is this meant to be:
But the sincere and baffled grief of one
Who walked with you under last summer's sun,
And laughed with you at vain mortality.
An hour, that afternoon, we sat for tea
In a café, upstairs. Time soon had run.
We talked of great things waiting to be done,—
Talking, as young men will, ambitiously.
I smiled, then, seeing your open throat, soft tie,
The golden, godlike head, your eyes' bold blue,
Your burning seriousness,—O youth! thought I.
But now (not strange), I think and think of you
Saying that day, 'It does not matter why
Men act: what matters most is what men do.'

The Valley of the Shadow

BY *Edwin Arlington Robinson*

There were faces to remember in the Valley of the Shadow,
There were faces unregarded, there were faces to forget;
There were fires of grief and fear that are a few forgotten ashes,
There were sparks of recognition that are not forgotten yet.
For at first, with an amazed and overwhelming indignation
At a measureless malfeasance that obscurely willed it thus,
They were lost and unacquainted—till they found themselves in others,
Who had groped as they were groping where dim ways were perilous.

There were lives that were as dark as are the fears and intuitions
Of a child who knows himself and is alone with what he knows;
There were pensioners of dreams and there were debtors of illusions,
All to fail before the triumph of a weed that only grows.
There were thirsting heirs of golden sieves that held not wine or water,
And had no names in traffic or more value there than toys:
There were blighted sons of wonder in the Valley of the Shadow,
Where they suffered and still wondered why their wonder made no noise.

There were slaves who dragged the shackles of a precedent unbroken,
Demonstrating the fulfillment of unalterable schemes,
Which had been, before the cradle, Time's inexorable tenants
Of what were now the dusty ruins of their father's dreams.

There were these, and there were many who had stumbled up to
manhood,
Where they saw too late the road they should have taken long ago:
There were thwarted clerks and fiddlers in the Valley of the Shadow,
The commemorative wreckage of what others did not know.

And there were daughters older than the mothers who had borne them,
Being older in their wisdom, which is older than the earth;
And they were going forward only farther into darkness,
Unrelieved as were the blasting obligations of their birth;
And among them, giving always what was not for their possession,
There were maidens, very quiet, with no quiet in their eyes:
There were daughters of the silence in the Valley of the Shadow,
Driven along in loving hundreds to the family sacrifice.

There were creepers among catacombs where dull regrets were torches,
Giving light enough to show them what there was upon the shelves—
Where there was more for them to see than pleasure would remember
Of something that had been alive and once had been themselves.
There were some who stirred the ruins with a solid imprecation,
While as many fled repentance for the promise of despair:
There were drinkers of wrong waters in the Valley of the Shadow,
And all the sparkling ways were dust that once had led them there.

There were some who knew the steps of Age incredibly beside them,
And his fingers upon shoulders that had never felt the wheel;
And their last of empty trophies was a gilded cup of nothing:

Which a contemplating vagabond would not have come to steal.
Long and often had they figured for a larger valuation,
But the size of their addition was the balance of a doubt:
There were gentlemen of leisure in the Valley of the Shadow,
Not allured by retrospection, disenchanted, and played out.

And among the dark endurances of unavowed reprisals
There were silent eyes of envy that saw little but saw well;
And over beauty's aftermath of hazardous ambitions
There were tears for what had vanished as they vanished where they fell.
Not assured of what was theirs, and always hungry for the nameless,
There were some whose only passion was for Time who made them cold:
There were numerous fair women in the Valley of the Shadow,
Dreaming rather less of heaven than of hell when they were old.

Now and then, as if to scorn the common touch of common sorrow,
There were some who gave a few the distant pity of a smile;
While another cloaked a soul as with an ash of human embers,
Having covered thus a treasure that would last him for a while.
There were many by the presence of the many disaffected,
Whose exemption was included in the weight that others bore:
There were seekers after darkness in the Valley of the Shadow,
And they alone were there to find what they were looking for.

There they were, and there they are; and as they came are coming others,
And among them are the fearless and the meek and the unborn;
And a question that has held us heretofore without an answer

May abide without an answer until all have ceased to mourn.
But the children of the dark are more to name than are the wretched,
Or the broken, or the weary, or the baffled, or the shamed:
There are builders of new mansions in the Valley of the Shadow,
And among them are the dying and the blinded and the maimed.

Foretaste

BY *Margaret Pond*

The sky stood up around me, blue,
Farther than sight, and then I knew
The river was a blue track curled
Through the pale centre of my world;
The mountains leaned against the sky,
Blue piled on blue, immensely high;
And in the sky a slant-winged bird
Moved slowly like a singing word.

Then as I drove I saw the road
Unwind blue miles; the river flowed
Implacable and strong and wide;
Lifting pale waves, a hurrying tide;
And trees grew up along its brim,
And higher towered the mesa's rim,
Drawing a black, unbroken line
Across blue sky, as clear as wine—
So clear I almost saw a star
Bright as infinity and far.

I was not body-bound this day.
The mountains pulled me clear away.
Upward I burned like their blue flame;
Then turned my eyes and quickly came
In one sharp flight to colored hills
Where no leaf grows. The black rain spills
Out of fierce clouds on silver days
And carves steep earth in curious ways;
And then I lay, a sage-swept plain
Slanting to riverward again.

I held low houses on my breast,
And wide church doors that opened west;
With simple folk I knelt and prayed,
And in their bodies long I stayed.
With their own hands I shaped warm earth
To bricks; and in swept rooms gave birth
To many a child, and saw some die;
I felt my breasts grow old and dry;
My tear-spent eyes were deep and wise
And sorrowless as star-edged skies;
At last I died and became earth
Close to the house that saw my birth.

And suddenly this curious thing,
Like spinning earth I seemed to sing;
A spinning earth I then became

And whirled through space like a blue flame.
Mountains were part of me and then
Made of the same flame I knew men.
Oh, then I saw what death might be,
What keen, unfettered ecstasy,
To be the earth, not just to see
Blue light spilled over hill and tree;
To feel the rain tread on my heart,
Not watch it shine, a thing apart,
And in all men to be the fire
Of grief and joy and quick desire.

My car moved slow. I felt the road
Weigh down upon me like a load.
I saw a woman, brown of face,
Hoeing hard earth with strong, sure grace;
I looked at her as at my friend;
I saw her turn from me and bend
Over her work. She did not know
I'd worn her flesh a while ago.
She did not even hear my cry.
Prisoned in body now was I.
I looked out on the gathering stars
As though my eyes were prison bars.

Litany for Dictatorships

BY *Stephen Vincent Benét*

For all those beaten, for the broken heads,
The fosterless, the simple, the oppressed,
The ghosts in the burning city of our time . . .

For those taken in rapid cars to the house and beaten
By the skillful boys, the boys with the rubber fists,
The boys who do it and like it and ask for more
—Held down and beaten, the table cutting their loins,
Or kicked in the groin and left, with the muscles jerking
Like a headless hen's on the floor of the slaughterhouse
While they brought the next man in with his white eyes staring.
For those who still said 'Red Front!' or 'God Save the Crown!'
And for those who were not courageous
But were beaten nevertheless.
For those who spit out the bloody stumps of their teeth
Quietly in the hall,
Sleep well on stone or iron, watch for the time
And kill the guard in the privy before they die,
Those with the deep-socketed eyes and the lamp burning.

For those who carry the scars, who walk lame—for those
Whose nameless graves are made in the prison yard
And the earth smoothed back before morning and the lime scattered.

For those slain at once. For those living through months and years
Enduring, watching, hoping, going each day
To the work or the queue for meat or the secret club,
Living meanwhile, begetting children, smuggling guns,
And found and killed at the end like rats in a drain.

For those escaping
Incredibly into exile and wandering there.
For those who live in the small rooms of foreign cities
And who yet think of the country, the long green grass,
The childhood voices, the language, the way wind smelt then,
The shape of rooms, the coffee drunk at the table,
The talk with friends, the loved city, the waiter's face,
The gravestones, with the name, where they will not lie
Nor in any of that earth. Their children are strangers.

For those who planned and were leaders and were beaten
And for those, humble and stupid, who had no plan
But were denounced, but grew angry, but told a joke,
But could not explain, but were sent away to the camp,
But had their bodies sent back in the sealed coffins,
'Died of pneumonia,' 'Died trying to escape.'

For those growers of wheat who were shot by their own wheat stacks.
For those growers of bread who were sent to the ice-locked wastes.
And their flesh remembers their fields.

For those denounced by their smug, horrible children
For a peppermint-star and the praise of the Perfect State.
For all those strangled or gelded or merely starved
To make perfect states; for the priest hanged in his cassock,
The Jew with his chest crushed in and his eyes dying,
The revolutionist lynched by the private guards
To make perfect states, in the names of the perfect states.

For those betrayed by the neighbors they shook hands with
And for the traitors, sitting in the hard chair
With the loose sweat crawling their hair and their fingers restless
As they tell the street and the house and the man's name.

And for those sitting at table in the house
With the lamp lit and the plates and the smell of food,
Talking so quietly; when they hear the cars
And the knock at the door, and they look at each other quickly
And the woman goes to the door with a stiff face,
Smoothing her dress.
                              'We are all good citizens here.
We believe in the Perfect State.'
                                        And that was the last
Time Tony or Karl or Shorty came to the house

And the family was liquidated later.
It was the last time.
                                        We heard the shots in the night
But nobody knew next day what the trouble was
And a man must go to his work. So I didn't see him
For three days, then, and me near out of my mind
And all the patrols on the streets with their dirty guns,
And when he came back he looked drunk, and the blood was on him.

For the women who mourn their dead in the secret night,
For the children taught to keep quiet, the old children,
The children spat on at school.
                                        For the wrecked laboratory,
The gutted house, the dunged picture, the spat-in well,
The naked corpse of Knowledge flung in the square
And no man lifting a hand and no man speaking.

For the cold of the pistol butt and the bullet's heat,
For the rope that chokes, the manacles that bind,
The huge voice, metal, that lies from a thousand tubes,
And the stuttering machine gun that answers all.

For the man crucified on the crossed machine guns
Without name, without resurrection, without stars,
His dark head heavy with death and his flesh long sour
With the smell of his many prisons—John Smith, John Doe,
John Nobody—oh, crack your mind for his name!

Faceless as water, naked as the dust,
Dishonored as the earth the gas shells poison,
And barbarous with portent.
                                        This is he.
This is the man they ate at the green table
Putting their gloves on ere they touched the meat.
This is the fruit of war, the fruit of peace,
The ripeness of invention, the new lamb,
The answer to the wisdom of the wise.
And still he hangs, and still he will not die,
And still, on the steel city of our years,
The light fails, and the terrible blood streams down.

We thought we were done with these things, but we were wrong.
We thought, because we had power, we had wisdom.
We thought the long train would run to the end of Time.
We thought the light would increase.
Now the long train stands derailed and the bandits loot it.
Now the boar and the asp have power in our time.
Now the night rolls back on the West and the night is solid.
Our fathers and ourselves sowed dragon's teeth.
Our children know and suffer the armed men.

Evening Meal in the Twentieth Century

BY *John Holmes*

How is it I can eat bread here and cut meat,
And in quiet shake salt, speak of the meal,
Pour water, serve my son's small plate?
Here now I love too well my wife's gold hair combed,
Her voice, her violin, our books on shelves in another room,
The tall chest shining darkly in supper-light.
I have read tonight
The sudden meaningless foreign violent death
Of a great man we both loved, hope
For a country not ours killed. But blacker than print:
For his million people no house now. For me
A new hurt to the old health of the heart once more:
That sore, that heavy, that dull and I think now incurable
Pain:
Seeing love hated, seeing real death,
Knowing evil alive I was taught was conquered.
How shall I cut this bread gladly, unless more share
The day's meals I earn?
Or offer my wife this meat from our fire, our fortune?
It should not have taken me so long to learn.
But how can I speak aloud at my own table tonight
And not curse my own food, not cry out death,
And not frighten my young son?

In Texas

BY *May Sarton*

In Texas the lid blew off the sky a long time ago,
So there's nothing to keep the wind from blowing
And it blows all the time. Everywhere is far to go,
So there's no hurry at all and no reason for going.
In Texas there's so much space words have a way
Of getting lost in the silence before they're spoken,
So people hang on a long time to what they have to say
And when they say it the silence is not broken,
But it absorbs the words and slowly gives them
Over to miles of white-gold plains and gray-green hills
And they are back in that silence that outlives them.
Nothing moves fast in Texas except the windmills
And the hawk that rises up with a clatter of wings.
(Nothing more startling here than sudden motion,
Everything is so still.) But the earth slowly swings
In time like a great swelling never-ending ocean,
And the houses that ride the tawny waves get smaller
As you get near them because you see them then
Under the whole sky, and the whole sky is so much taller
With the lid off than a million towers built by men.
After a while you can only see what's at horizon's edge,
And you are stretched with looking so far instead of near,

So you jump, you are startled by a blown piece of sedge,
You feel wide-eyed and ruminative as ponderous steer.
In Texas you look at America with a patient eye.
You want everything to be sure and slow and set in relation
To immense skies and earth that never ends. You wonder why
People must talk and strain so much about a nation
That lives in spaces vaster than a man's dream, can go
Five hundred miles through wilderness meeting only the hawk
And the dead rabbit on the road. What happens must be slow,
Must go deeper even than hand's work or tongue's talk,
Must rise out of the flesh like sweat after a hard day,
Must come slowly in its own time, in its own way.

Dark Symphony

BY *Melvin B. Tolson*

I

Allegro Moderato

Black Crispus Attucks taught
Us how to die
Before white Patrick Henry's bugle breath
Uttered the vertical
Transmitting cry:
'Yea, give me liberty, or give me death.'

And from that day to this
Men black and strong
For Justice and Democracy have stood,
Steeled in the faith that Right
Will conquer Wrong
And Time will usher in one brotherhood.

No Banquo's ghost can rise
Against us now
And say we crushed men with a tyrant's boot,
Or pressed the crown of thorns
On Labor's brow,
Or ravaged lands and carted off the loot.

II

Lento Grave

The centuries-old pathos in our voices
Saddens the great white world,
And the wizardry of our dusky rhythms
Conjures up shadow-shapes of ante-bellum years:

Black slaves singing *One More River to Cross*
In the torture tombs of slave-ships,
Black slaves singing *Steal Away to Jesus*
In jungle swamps,

Black slaves singing *The Crucifixion*
In slave-pens at midnight,
Black slaves singing *Swing Low, Sweet Chariot*
In cabins of death,
Black slaves singing *Go Down, Moses*
In the canebrakes of the Southern Pharaohs.

III

Andante Sostenuto

They tell us to forget
The Golgotha we tread . . .
We who are scourged with hate,
A price upon our head.
They who have shackled us
Require of us a song,

They who have wasted us
Bid us o'erlook the wrong.

They tell us to forget
Democracy is spurned.
They tell us to forget
The Bill of Rights is burned.
Three hundred years we slaved,
We slave and suffer yet:
Though flesh and bone rebel,
They tell us to forget!

Oh, how can we forget
Our human rights denied?
Oh, how can we forget
Our manhood crucified?
When Justice is profaned
And plea with curse is met,
When Freedom's gates are barred,
Oh, how can we forget?

IV

Tempo Primo

The New Negro strides upon the continent
In seven-league boots . . .
The New Negro
Who sprang from the vigor-stout loins

Of Nat Turner, gallows-martyr for Freedom,
Of Joseph Cinquez, Black Moses of the Amistad Mutiny,
Of Frederick Douglass, oracle of the Catholic Man,
Of Sojourner Truth, eye and ear of Lincoln's legions,
Of Harriet Tubman, Saint Bernard of the Underground Railroad.

The New Negro
Breaks the icons of his detractors,
Wipes out the conspiracy of silence,
Speaks to his America:

My history-moulding ancestors
Planted the first crops of wheat on these shores,
Built ships to conquer the seven seas,
Erected the Cotton Empire,
Flung railroads across a hemisphere,
Disemboweled the earth's iron and coal,
Tunneled the mountains and bridged rivers,
Harvested the grain and hewed forests,
Sentineled the Thirteen Colonies,
Unfurled Old Glory at the North Pole,
Fought a hundred battles for the Republic.

The New Negro:
His giant hands fling murals upon high chambers,
His drama teaches a world to laugh and weep,
His music leads continents captive,

His voice thunders the Brotherhood of Labor,
His science creates seven wonders,
His Republic of Letters challenges the Negro-baiters.

The New Negro,
Hard-muscled, Fascist-hating, Democracy-ensouled,
Strides in seven-league boots
Along the Highway of Today
Toward the Promised Land of Tomorrow!

V

Larghetto

None in the Land can say
To us black men Today:
You send the tractors on their bloody path,
And create Okies for *The Grapes of Wrath*.
You breed the slum that breeds a *Native Son*
To damn the good earth Pilgrim Fathers won.

None in the Land can say
To us black men Today:
You dupe the poor with rags-to-riches tales,
And leave the workers empty dinner pails.
You stuff the ballot box, and honest men
Are muzzled by your demagogic din.

None in the Land can say
To us black men Today:
You smash stock markets with your coined blitzkriegs,
And make a hundred million guinea pigs.
You counterfeit our Christianity,
And bring contempt upon Democracy.

None in the Land can say
To us black men Today:
You prowl when citizens are fast asleep,
And hatch Fifth Column plots to blast the deep
Foundations of the State and leave the Land
A vast Sahara with a Fascist brand.

None in the Land can say
To us black men Today:
You send flame-gutting tanks like swarms of flies,
And plump a hell from dynamiting skies.
You fill machine-gunned towns with rotting dead—
A No Man's Land where children cry for bread.

VI

Tempo di Marcia

Out of abysses of Illiteracy,
Through labyrinths of Lies,
Across wastelands of Disease . . .
We advance!

Out of dead-ends of Poverty,
Through wildernesses of Superstition,
Across barricades of Jim Crowism . . .
We advance!

With the Peoples of the World . . .
We advance!

Pacific Lament

BY *Charles Olson*

IN MEMORY OF WILLIAM HICKEY, A MEMBER OF THE CREW OF THE U.S.S. GROWLER, LOST AT SEA IN FEBRUARY, 1944.

Black at that depth
turn, golden boy no more
white bone to bone, turn
hear who bore you weep
hear him who made you
deep there on ocean's floor
turn
as waters stir;
turn, bone of man

Cold as a planet is
cold, beat of blood no more
the salt sea's course
along the bone jaw white
stir, boy, stir
motion without motion
stir, and hear
love come down.

Down as you fell
sidewise, stair to green stair
without breath, down
the tumble of ocean
to find you, bone
cold and new among the ships
and men and fish askew.

You alone o golden boy no more
turn now and sleep
washed white by water
sleep in your black deep
by water out of which man came
to find his legs, arms, love, pain.
Sleep, boy, sleep
in older arms than hers,
rocked by an older father;
toss no more,
love;
sleep.

Skyscraper Canticle

BY *Carl Sandburg*

Bless Thee, O Lord, for the living arc of the sky over me this
morning.
Bless Thee, O Lord, for the companionship of night mist far above
the skyscraper tops I saw when I woke once during the night.
Bless Thee, O Lord, for the miracle of light to my eyes and the
involved mystery of it that I do not expect to solve so long
as I live.
Bless Thee, O Lord, for the laws Thou hast ordained that hold these
tall buildings together and that govern the planet Earth in
its course and farther away the cycle of the Sun.

Frederick Douglass

BY *Robert E. Hayden*

When it is finally ours, this freedom, this liberty, this beautiful
and terrible thing, needful to man as air,
usable as the earth; when it belongs at last to our children,
when it is truly instinct, brain-matter, diastole, systole,
reflex action; when it is finally won; when it is more
than the gaudy mumbo-jumbo of politicians:
this man, this Douglass, this former slave, this Negro
beaten to his knees, exiled, visioning a world
where none is lonely, none hunted, alien,
this man, superb in love and logic, this man
shall be remembered—oh, not with statues' rhetoric,
not with legends and poems and wreaths of bronze alone,
but with the lives grown out of his life, the lives
fleshing his dream of the needful, beautiful thing.

For the Union Dead

BY *Robert Lowell*

Relinquunt omnia servare rem publicam.

The old South Boston Aquarium stands
in a Sahara of snow now. Its broken windows are boarded.
The bronze weathervane cod has lost half its scales.
The airy tanks are dry.

Once my nose crawled like a snail on the glass;
my hand tingled
to burst the bubbles,
drifting from the noses of the cowed, compliant fish.

My hand draws back. I often sigh still
for the dark downward and vegetating kingdom
of the fish and reptile. One morning last March,
I pressed against the new barbed and galvanized

fence on the Boston Common. Behind their cage,
yellow dinosaur steam shovels were grunting
as they cropped up tons of mush and grass
to gouge their underworld garage.

Parking lots luxuriate like civic
sand piles in the heart of Boston.
A girdle of orange, Puritan-pumpkin-colored girders
braces the tingling Statehouse, shaking

over the excavations, as it faces Colonel Shaw
and his bell-cheeked Negro infantry
on St. Gaudens' shaking Civil War relief,
propped by a plank splint against the garage's earthquake.

Two months after marching through Boston,
half the regiment was dead;
at the dedication,
William James could almost hear the bronze Negroes breathe.

The monument sticks like a fishbone
in the city's throat.
Its colonel is as lean
as a compass needle.

He has an angry wrenlike vigilance,
a greyhound's gentle tautness;
he seems to wince at pleasure
and suffocate for privacy.

He is out of bounds. He rejoices in man's lovely,
peculiar power to choose life and die—

when he leads his black soldiers to death,
he cannot bend his back.

On a thousand small-town New England greens,
the old white churches hold their air
of sparse, sincere rebellion; frayed flags
quilt the graveyards of the Grand Army of the Republic.

The stone statues of the abstract Union Soldier
grow slimmer and younger each year—
wasp-waisted, they doze over muskets,
and muse through their sideburns.

Shaw's father wanted no monument
except the ditch,
where his son's body was thrown
and lost with his "niggers."

The ditch is nearer.
There are no statues for the last war here;
on Boylston Street, a commercial photograph
showed Hiroshima boiling

over a Mosler Safe, "the Rock of Ages,"
that survived the blast. Space is nearer.
When I crouch to my television set,
the drained faces of Negro school children rise like balloons.

Colonel Shaw
is riding on his bubble,
he waits
for the blessed break.

The Aquarium is gone. Everywhere,
giant finned cars nose forward like fish;
a savage servility
slides by on grease.

One Day

BY *Jeannette Nichols*

One day
like no other
Vermont
undefined in early mists
into which we woke
in a tent
my Father and I
and moved in our damp bones
around woodsmoke
while the mists burned away
and three crows flew over
knowing everything;

one morning like no other
my Father with eyes full of woodsmoke and tears
and I
trampling Vermont's indistinct wet grass
saw those crows fly over
in dry dark shapes,
felt three
flickering shadows
cross our faces
as quick as love.

A Good View from Flagstaff

BY *Richard Hugo*

Let's take it as it is: acres flowing
yellow north and people so small in the distance
we believe them happy working fields.
Despite the heat, the sun is less than cruel.
Soil is wet black and the wheat rolls far enough
to be a lemon sea. Silos waver
and are silver salmon two wines into lunch.

This view is what one needs to love the world
when things go bad. Take Naples, '67, me alone
in Vomero, no sleep for nights, endless sweat,
my system out of chemical whack from weeks
of suicidal drinking and the sad scenes of my life
locked with me in the hotel room like bats.
Far off, through my window, a white apartment
building gleamed each morning and I knew
out there beyond me somewhere was a world
worth having because it caught the sun
and sent the light back to the sea confirmed.
Because it sat there quiet far away.

A good view here. We ignore the mean acts
in the houses though we can't forget they go on
daily with the soul's attrition. We are certain
why the plow horse limps. Spread the way it is
by wind, the world in cultivated patchwork
claims we travel on the right freight one day
and the years are gone. At worst
they're more than nothing. The best friends
we remember took us home the way we are.

Welcome to Hiroshima

BY *Mary Jo Salter*

is what you see first, stepping off the train:
a billboard brought to you in living English
by Toshiba Electric. While a channel
silent in the TV of the brain

projects those flickering re-runs of a cloud
that brims its risen columnful like beer
and, spilling over, hangs its foamy head,
you feel a thirst for history: what year

it started to be safe to breathe the air,
and when to drink the blood and scum clogging
the Ohta River. But no, the water's clear,
they pour it for your morning cup of tea

in one of the countless sunny coffee shops
which advertise with plastic dioramas
mutations of cuisine behind the glass:
a pancake sandwich; a pizza someone tops

with a maraschino cherry. Passing by
the Peace Park's floral hypocenter (where

how bravely, or with what mistaken cheer,
humanity erased its own erasure)

you enter the memorial museum
and, through more glass, are served up on a bed
of blistered grass three mannequins. Like gloves
a mother clips to coatsleeves, strings of flesh

hang from their fingertips. Or as if tied
to recall a duty, *Reverence the dead*
whose rememberers shall also soon be dead,
but instead that hunger's swallowed up in taste,

questions of bad discernment, the mock display
of images that remain unparalleled—
and thinking at last *They should have left it all*
you stop. This is the wristwatch of a child

jammed at the moment of impact. Resolute
to communicate some message, although mute,
it gestures with its hands at eight-fifteen
and eight-fifteen and eight-fifteen again

while tables of statistics on the wall
update the news by calling on a roll
of tape, death gummed on death, and in the case
adjacent, an exhibit under glass

is glass itself: a shard the bomb slammed in
a woman's arm at eight-fifteen, but some
three decades on—as if to make it plain
hope's only as renewable as pain

and as if all the unsung
debasements of the past may one day come
rising to the surface once again—
worked its filthy way out like a tongue.

The Baseball Players

BY *Donald Hall*

Against the bright
grass the white-knickered
players tense, seize,
and attend. A moment
ago, outfielders
and infielders adjusted
their clothing, glanced
at the sun and settled
forward, hands on knees;
the catcher twitched
a forefinger; the pitcher
walked back of the hill,
established his cap,
and returned; the batter
rotated his bat
in a slow circle.
                    But now
they pause: wary,
exact, suspended—
while abiding moonrise
lightens the angel
of the overgrown
garden, and Walter Blake
Adams, who died
at fourteen, waits
under the footbridge.

Sunday in the Old Republic

BY *Derek Walcott*

Where a cathedral shows
the sun-sliced orange face,
windows fanned and roseace,
and a black-tasseled carriage

clops from past centuries
through the black iron gates
of the park that breathes
through those ribs, maids

curse their stumbling kids
near the artificial lakes
floating with strolling crowds
of lilies, a bearded fin-de-siècle

likes to sit on the iron curl
of a carved bench. Silk hats,
clouds' crumpled linen coats
and dragonflies whose gauze

wings fade like rainbows.
Lies. It was never like this.
There never was any peace
in the spin of parasols;

their peace only exists
in the leaf-shadowed prose
of the imaginary Republic, its
Impressionist canvases.

Down the path, the old peach-
colored path, a soldier's
barrel-organ goes, a pouch
on one eye, and a marmoset

with questioning tail and eyes
that seem always amazed
at the chain around its waist
or at the nurses' cries

at children on the edge
of the darkening pasture
where a swan and her cygnets
sail faster and faster

down the cold current.

Powers of Congress

BY *Alice Fulton*

How the lightstruck trees change sun
to flamepaths: veins, sap, stem, all
on brief loan, set to give all
their spooled, coded heat to stoves called
Resolute: wet steel diecast
by heat themselves. Tree, beast, bug—
the worldclass bit parts in this
world—flit and skid through it; the
powers of congress tax, spend, law
what lives to pure crisp form
then break forms' lock, stock, and hold
on flesh. All night couples pledge
to stay flux, the hit-run stuff
of cracked homes. Men trim their quick
lawns each weekend, trailing power
mowers. Heartslaves, you've seen them: wives
with flexed hair, hitched to bored kids,
twiddling in good living rooms,
their twin beds slept in, changed, made.

Used

BY *Rita Dove*

The conspiracy's to make us thin. Size three's
all the rage, and skirts ballooning above twinkling knees
are every man-child's pre-adolescent dream.
Tabula rasa. No slate's *that* clean—

we've earned the navels sunk in grief
when the last child emptied us of their brief
interior light. Our muscles say *We have been used.*

Have you ever tried silk sheets? I did,
persuaded by post-natal dread
and a Macy's clerk to bargain for more zip.
We couldn't hang on, slipped
to the floor and by morning the quilts
had slid off, too. Enough of guilt—
It's hard work staying cool.

Among Children

BY *Philip Levine*

I walk among the rows of bowed heads—
the children are sleeping through fourth grade
so as to be ready for what is ahead,
the monumental boredom of junior high
and the rush forward tearing their wings
loose and turning their eyes forever inward.
These are the children of Flint, their fathers
work at the spark plug factory or truck
bottled water in five-gallon sea-blue jugs
to the widows of the suburbs. You can see
already how their backs have thickened,
how their small hands, soiled by pig iron,
leap and stutter even in dreams. I would like
to sit down among them and read slowly
from the Book of Job until the windows
pale and the teacher rises out of a milky sea
of industrial scum, her gowns streaming
with light, her foolish words transformed
into song, I would like to arm each one
with a quiver of arrows so that they might
rush like wind there where no battle rages
shouting among the trumpets, Ha! Ha!

How dear the gift of laughter in the face
of the eight-hour day, the cold winter mornings
without coffee and oranges, the long lines
of mothers in old coats waiting silently
where the gates have closed. Ten years ago
I went among these same children, just born,
in the bright ward of the Sacred Heart and leaned
down to hear their breaths delivered that day,
burning with joy. There was such wonder
in their sleep, such purpose in their eyes
closed against autumn, in their damp heads
blurred with the hair of ponds, and not one
turned against me or the light, not one
said, I am sick, I am tired, I will go home,
not one complained or drifted alone,
unloved, on the hardest day of their lives.
Eleven years from now they will become
the men and women of Flint or Paradise,
the majors of a minor town, and I
will be gone into smoke or memory,
so I bow to them here and whisper
all I know, all I will never know.

Darling

BY *Naomi Shihab Nye*

1

I break this toast for the ghost of bread in Lebanon.
The split stone, the toppled doorway.

Someone's kettle has been crushed.
Someone's sister has a gash above her right eye.

And now our tea has trouble being sweet.
A strawberry softens, turns musty,

overnight each apple grows a bruise.
I tie both shoes on Lebanon's feet.

All day the sky in Texas which has seen no rain since June
is raining Lebanese mountains, Lebanese trees.

What if the air grew damp with the names of mothers,
the clear belled voices of first-graders

pinned to the map of Lebanon like a shield?
When I visited the camp of the opposition

near the lonely Golan, looking northward toward
Syria and Lebanon, a vine was springing pinkly from a tin can

and a woman with generous hips like my mother's
said Follow me.

2

Someone was there.
Someone not there now was standing.
Someone in the wrong place
with a small moon-shaped scar on his left cheek
and a boy by the hand.

Who had just drunk water, sharing the glass.
Who had not thought about it deeply
though they might have, had they known.
Someone grown and someone not-grown.
Who thought they had different amounts of time left.
This guessing game ends with our hands in the air,
becoming air.
One who was there is not there, for no reason.
Two who were there.

It was almost too big to see.

3

Our friend from Turkey says language is so delicate
he likens it to a darling.

We will take this word in our arms.
It will be small and breathing.
We will not wish to scare it.
Pressing lips to the edge of each syllable.
Nothing else will save us now.
The word "together" wants to live in every house.

Jersey Rain

BY *Robert Pinsky*

Now near the end of the middle stretch of road
What have I learned? Some earthly wiles. An art.
That often I cannot tell good fortune from bad,
That once had seemed so easy to tell apart.

The source of art and woe aslant in wind
Dissolves or nourishes everything it touches.
What roadbank gullies and ruts it doesn't mend
It carves the deeper, boiling tawny in ditches.

It spends itself regardless into the ocean.
It stains and scours and makes things dark or bright:
Sweat of the moon, a shroud of benediction,
The chilly liquefaction of day to night,

The Jersey rain, my rain, soaks all as one:
It smites Metuchen, Rahway, Saddle River,
Fair Haven, Newark, Little Silver, Bayonne.
I feel it churning even in fair weather

To craze distinction, dry the same as wet.
In ripples of heat the August drought still feeds
Vapors in the sky that swell to smite the state—
The Jersey rain, my rain, in streams and beads

Of indissoluble grudge and aspiration:
Original milk, replenisher of grief,
Descending destroyer, arrowed source of passion,
Silver and black, executioner, font of life.

Martin Luther King Jr. Mourns Trayvon Martin

BY *Lauren K. Alleyne*

For you, son,
I dreamed a childhood
unburdened by hate;
a boyhood of adventure—
skinned knees and hoops,
first loves and small rebellions;
I dreamed you whole
and growing into your own
manhood, writing its definitions
with your daily being.
I dreamed you alive, living.

For you, America's African heir,
I dreamed a future
of open doors, of opportunity
without oppression,
of affirmation and action,
I dreamed Oprah and Obama
I dreamed Colin and Condoleezza
I dreamed doctors and dancers,
lawyers and linebackers, models,
musicians, mechanics, preachers
and professors and police, authors,

activists, astronauts, even,
all black as Jesus is.

I dreamed you dapper—
the black skin of you
polished to glow; your curls,
your kinks, your locs,
your bald, your wild,
your freshly barbered—
all beautiful.

I dreamed you wearing whatever the hell you want
and not dying for it.

For you, brother,
I dreamed a world softened
by love, free from the fear
that makes too-early ancestors of our men;
turns our boys into targets,
headlines, and ghosts.

I had a dream
that my children will one day live
in a nation where they will not be judged
by the color of their skin
but by the content of their character.
Sweet song of my sorrow.

Sweet dream, deferred.
For you, gone one, I dreamed
justice—her scales tipped
away from your extinction,
her eyes and arms unbound
and open to you
at last.

The Coal Cellar

BY *Nikki Giovanni*

Electricity was late and expensive
Coming to Appalachia
Knoxville especially so
Twice a month the coal
Man would come to fill the cellar
For warmth and sometimes food
And what I loved most was the fireplace
Where Grandmother and Grandpapa would sit
Near to tell stories but
Oak Ridge came for the war
Or maybe the war came for Oak Ridge
And atomic energy replaced coal
And the cellar became a home for mice
And maybe some insects that we never
Needed to bother since they didn't bother us

One summer day Grandmother said
To me, "Since John Brown will be gone
For the conference why don't we see what
Is in the cellar"
I didn't think anything but if your grandmother
Asks you to go cellaring with her
You go

Way to the front she pulled a box out
And handed it to me
"See? I thought it would still be here"
And we climbed out and up or maybe up and out
And into the kitchen where we were both dripping
With ash
"This belongs to your great grandmother
Cornelia
The first person born free"
And there was a sterling silver dinner spoon and fork
Black as can be but properly hallmarked

"I'll let you polish them"

Which I did though it took
Several days
To bring them to silver

I'll bet there are many precious
Things in the cellars
Of Appalachia
The most being the trust my grandmother
Had in me to keep the silver polished
And not discussed with anyone

Maybe not a big bank account or trust fund
And certainly not any property but I inherited
A morning and a great deal of knowledge
In a cold coal cellar
With my grandmother

Benediction

BY *Joshua Bennett*

God bless the lightning
bolt in my little
brother's hair.
God bless our neighborhood
barber, the patience it takes
to make a man
you've just met
beautiful. God bless
every beautiful thing
called monstrous
since the dawn
of a colonizer's time.
God bless the arms
of the mother
on the cross
-town bus, the sterling silver
cross at the crux
of her collarbone, its shine
barely visible beneath her nightshade
-navy New York
Yankees hoodie.
God bless the baby boy

kept precious
in her embrace.
His wail turning
my entire row
into an opera house.
God bless the vulnerable
ones. How they call us
toward love & its infinite,
unthinkable costs.
God bless the floss.
The flash. The brash
& bare-knuckle brawl
of the South Bronx girls
who raised my mother
to grease knuckles, cut eyes,
get fly as any fugitive dream
on the lam,
on the run
from the Law
as any & all of us are
who dare to wake
& walk in this
skin & you
best believe
God blessed
this skin,
the shimmer & slick

of it, the wherewithal
to bear the rage of brothers,
sisters slain & still function
each morning, still
sit at a desk, send
an email, take an order,
dream a world, some heaven
big enough for black life
to flourish, to grow, God
bless the *no*, my story
is not for sale
the *no*, this body
belongs to me & the earth
alone, the *see*, the thing
about souls
is they by definition
cannot be owned God
bless the beloved flesh
our refusal calls
home God bless the unkillable
interior bless the uprising
bless the rebellion bless
the overflow God
bless everything that survives
the fire

The Wish

BY *Dong Li*

once again
of not coming
to know
the strident
sorrows
unfulfilled for
fatherland
of not seeing
loved ones
their remains
drifted
in the far earth
of saying father
father and to be
heard
in this benign
beginning
a gray sky
a fleet
of nonbirds
of faces
of inaudible

singsongs
not a word
unrecognizable
atoned in this
despicable pit
of a large burning
once and for all
again a face
your face
flies
into nothing
the wish
never to be
in-
visible

Nostrand and Lincoln

BY *Janelle Tan*

in the crown fried chicken, the toilet seat lifted by a shelf,
nikes line the bathroom wall—

the cooks in their rubber slippers
call out another order.

our feet make us immigrants
before a first winter.

outside the small home
of this bathroom,

one of the cooks says, *love you, bro*,
rubbing the other cook's forehead as he leaves for the night.

i love you, i say to you, and you, and you,
as i leave the bar.

in our living room above the crown fried chicken
you tell me, *it's aerodynamics*—

the birds in front break the air
so the ones behind them face less resistance.

the birds individual, then
a collective,

rearranging themselves
so every bird can rest.

all i know about leaving a place
to land somewhere else

is defiance.
american desire.

my friend who lives in a basement apartment
with no windows and no light

tells me it is all worth it
because of the people she's met in this city.

the immigrant quashing
of longing—
yet another door

cracked open,
the small sliver of light

we are taught to call home.

once, after i hugged you goodnight,
i asked the cook at crown fried chicken,

when do you rest?—he said,
if i rest, who will feed all of you?

every day we build
our homes

in another man's heaven.

II.

NATURAL LINES

Sonnet

BY *James Russell Lowell*

The Maple puts her corals on in May,
While loitering frosts about the lowlands cling,
To be in tune with what the robins sing,
Plastering new log-huts 'mid her branches gray;
But when the Autumn southward turns away,
Then in her veins burns most the blood of Spring,
And every leaf, intensely blossoming,
Makes the year's sunset pale the set of day.
O Youth unprescient, were it only so
With trees you plant, and in whose shade reclined,
Thinking their drifting blooms Fate's coldest snow,
You carve dear names upon the faithful rind,
Nor in that vernal stem the cross foreknow
That Age may bear, silent, yet unresigned!

A Summer Day

BY *Celia Thaxter*

At daybreak, in the fresh light, joyfully
The fishermen drew in their laden net;
The shore shone rosy purple, and the sea
Was streaked with violet,

And, pink with sunrise, many a shadowy sail
Lay southward, lighting up the sleeping bay,
And in the west the white moon, still and pale,
Faded before the day.

Silence was everywhere. The rising tide
Slowly filled every cove and inlet small:
A musical low whisper, multiplied,
You heard, and that was all.

No clouds at dawn,—but, as the sun climbed higher,
White columns, thunderous, splendid, up the sky
Floated and stood, heaped in the sun's clear fire,
A stately company.

Stealing along the coast from cape to cape,
  The weird mirage crept tremulously on,
In many a magic change and wondrous shape,
          Throbbing beneath the sun.

At noon the wind rose,—swept the glassy sea
  To sudden ripple,—thrust against the clouds
A strenuous shoulder,—gathering steadily,
          Drove them before in crowds,

Till all the west was dark, and inky black
  The level ruffled water underneath,
And up the wind-cloud tossed, a ghostly rack,
          In many a ragged wreath.

Then sudden roared the thunder, a great peal
  Magnificent, that broke and rolled away;
And down the wind plunged, like a furious keel
          Cleaving the sea to spray,

And brought the rain, sweeping o'er land and sea.
  And then was tumult! Lightning, sharp and keen,
Thunder, wind, rain,—a mighty jubilee
          The heaven and earth between!

And loud the ocean sang,—a chorus grand,—
   A solemn music sung in undertone
Of waves that broke about, on either hand,
            The little island lone,

Where, joyful in His tempest as His calm,
   Held in the hollow of that hand of His,
I joined with heart and soul in God's great psalm,
            Thrilled with a nameless bliss.

Soon lulled the wind,—the summer storm soon died;
   The shattered clouds went eastward, drifting slow;
From the low sun the rain-fringe swept aside,
            Bright in his rosy glow,

And wide a splendor streamed through all the sky
   O'er land and sea one soft, delicious blush,
That touched the gray rocks lightly, tenderly,
            A transitory flush.

Warm, odorous gusts came off the distant land,
   With spice of pine-woods, breath of hay new-mown,
O'er miles of waves and sea-scents cool and bland,
            Full in our faces blown.

Slow faded the sweet light, and peacefully
  The quiet stars came out, one after one,—
The holy twilight deepened silently,
          The summer day was done.

Such unalloyed delight its hours had given,
  Musing, this thought rose in my grateful mind,
That God, who watches all things, up in heaven,
          With patient eyes and kind,

Saw and was pleased, perhaps, one child of His
  Dared to be happy like the little birds,
Because He gave His children days like this,
          Rejoicing beyond words,—

Dared, lifting up to Him untroubled eyes
  In gratitude that worship is, and prayer,
Sing and be glad with ever new surprise
          He made His world so fair!

Madrigal

BY *Howard Glyndon (Laura Redden Searing)*

Every robin-redbreast takes himself a mate!
Say the birds, sing the birds, "It is wrong to wait
Till the lily-footed spring glides out at summer's gate."
So I heard the birds sing, once upon a day:
O, my treasure! O, my pleasure! Canst thou say me nay?

Birds' songs and birds' nests and green boughs together,
All gone: love alone laughs at bitter weather.
Summer days or winter days; little recks Love whether;
If so be that Love have his own, his darling way.
Ah, my fairest! Ah, my rarest! Canst thou say me nay?

In the wood the wind-flower is sunken out of sight,
Low down and deep down and world-forgotten quite.
But do you think the Wind forgets that she was sweet and white?
Then listen to his sad voice a little while, I pray!
O, my cruel! O, my jewel! Canst thou say me nay?

The sun stole to a red rose and wiled her leaves apart:
May dew and June air had wooed her at the start;
But was't not fair the sun should have her golden, perfect heart?
Let me choose one short word for timid lips to say:
Ah, my precious! My delicious! It shall not be nay!

The Breakers

BY *Charles Washington Coleman*

A pulsing organ-toned arpeggio,
Crescendo mounting, with a sweep sublime;
A swift back-rushing of diminished sound,
A gasp for breath, a futile long-drawn sigh;
A momentary hush, with cries of gulls
Struck through and through, staccato; then the roar
Of great swift chords, that crash and break and blend,
A sobbing undertone, marked by the hiss
Of yellow foam left stranded in the sun.
And then da capo.

Tiger-Lilies

BY *Michael Field*

Lilies, are you come!
I quail before you as your buds upswell;
        It is the miracle
Of fire and sculpture in your brazen urns
        That strikes me dumb,—
Fire of midsummer that burns,
        And as it passes,
Flinging rich sparkles on its own clear blaze,
Wreathes with the wreathing tongues and rays,
Great tiger-lilies, of your deep-cleft masses!
        It is the wonder
        I am laid under
        By the firm heaves
And over-tumbling edges of your liberal leaves.

Birches

BY *Robert Frost*

When I see birches bend to left and right
Across the lines of straighter darker trees,
I like to think some boy's been swinging them.
But swinging doesn't bend them down to stay.
Ice-storms do that. Often you must have seen them
Loaded with ice a sunny winter morning
After a rain. They click upon themselves
As the breeze rises, and turn many-colored
As the stir cracks and crazes their enamel.
Soon the sun's warmth makes them shed crystal shells
Shattering and avalanching on the snow-crust—
Such heaps of broken glass to sweep away
You'd think the inner dome of heaven had fallen.
They are dragged to the withered bracken by the load
And they seem not to break; though once they are bowed
So low for long they never right themselves:
You may see their trunks arching in the woods
Years afterwards, trailing their leaves on the ground
Like girls on hands and knees that throw their hair
Before them over their heads to dry in the sun.

But I was going to say when truth broke in
With all her matter-of-fact about the ice-storm,
(Now am I free to be poetical?)
I should prefer to have some boy bend them
As he went out and in to fetch the cows—
Some boy too far from town to learn baseball,
Whose only play was what he found himself,
Summer or winter, and could play alone.
One by one he subdued his father's trees
By riding them down over and over again
Until he took the stiffness out of them
And not one but hung limp, not one was left
For him to conquer. He learned all there was
To learn about not launching out too soon
And so not carrying the tree away
Clear to the ground. He always kept his poise
To the top branches, climbing carefully
With the same pains you use to fill a cup
Up to the brim, and even above the brim.
Then he flung outward, feet first, with a swish,
Kicking his way down through the air to the ground.
So was I once myself a swinger of birches.
And so I dream of going back to be.
It's when I'm weary of considerations,
And life is too much like a pathless wood
Where your face burns and tickles with the cobwebs
Broken across it, and one eye is weeping

From a twig's having lashed across it open.
I'd like to get away from earth awhile
And then come back to it and begin over.
May no fate willfully misunderstand me
And half grant what I wish and snatch me away
Not to return. Earth's the right place for love:
I don't know where it's likely to go better.
I'd like to go by climbing a birch tree,
And climb black branches up a snow-white trunk
Toward heaven, till the tree could bear no more,
But dipped its top and set me down again.
That would be good both going and coming back.
One could do worse than be a swinger of birches.

Beauty Is Gathered Like the Rain on Hills

BY *Dorothy Leonard*

Beauty is gathered like the rain on hills:
  Here sinking into reservoirs of moss,
    Whose beryl stars are guardians of loss,
And there a cowslip-hidden pool it fills.
Or if, uncisterned by the earth, it spills
  In thin cascades where staircased ledges cross
    A lonely hill-road, careless, cold winds toss
Its spray on granite fields that no man tills.

Diminish as it may, or disappear
  From barren pastures, beauty cannot fail
    While there are crevices to drink its dew.
  Following, following down, like springs in shale
    Or vanished old sea-sand, it filters through
Lost littorals of dream, and issues clear.

Autumn Evening

BY *Jean Batchelor*

Here is a world where everything is shifting,
A fading world beneath the fading splendor
Of evening earlier than yesterday,
Darker and earlier. The night too soon
Chilling an earth still stubble-warm with summer
Settles like dust, like death, upon these meadows.
Cool light slips over them, light still slips over
On slowly flowing air; brightness still brims
Clear pools of air between the drifting shadows,
The leaf's edge and the cloud's edge still are bright,
But all is darkening, all will dim and darken
And ebb away to evening, ebb to autumn.
Without a sound, without a lapping ripple
Summer flows past, flows out upon the wind
Under the darkening sky. A flight of shadows
Up from the ground takes wing, and in the branches
Dark shapes among dark boughs give out a cry,
The windy cry of crows, as if the autumn
Spoke in their throats, a sound of cold and darkness,
The sound of winter wind in leafless woods.

Return

BY *Josephine W. Johnson*

The alien, tortured mind goes back,
Recalls those quiet hills, the falling apricots, the quail.

Returns to that still valley in the night,
The white thorn apples in the dark,
The wild white clover in the sun.

There quiet and changeless in those pastures,
The warm white oat fields and the cold sweet corn,
Ends the black spirit's eyeless flight,
Ends the black fever, and the fever's light,
Dies in the slow leaf-searching sound of rain.

Under the white stars and the silence,
Walking the cold grass of those hills,
The dry leaf lives, the monster dies,
The savage heart that knows its own
Grows still.

Northeast Coast

BY *Frances Frost*

The light fell and diminished:
it was the end of light.
The sea moved colored till purple and flame were finished
at the edge of night.

It was the first of dark,
the last of day,
the verge of visible stars, the merge of hours
when space grew wounded with piercing and turning flowers.
Over the quiet bay

the gulls went north as in forgotten Springs
to island gatherings. . . .
(They would return with morning, scream and ride
in the cold sea-hush,
float and quarrel on the rising tide,
until the final rush
of sun should blind the continent.)

But now
they darkened past the twisted cedar boughs,
they cut the lucid air
with narrow wings abruptly bound
to rocks we never knew and shall not know.
(O secret and washed by midnight waters, bare
save for the weight of wild and drowsy wings!)

The constellations, as in other Springs,
burst like buds on the sky's dark tree, the air
quivered with living worlds. The coast was lonely,
humped with scrub and fern, thrusting its shale
into the spatter of foam, the dark-moon shock. . . .
The lifting tide sobbed only; you were not there.
It was the shore we loved, it was the near
sea-throat.

(The cricket, invisible and clear,
sharpened Autumn in the half-grown grass.)

July Mountain

BY *Wallace Stevens*

We live in a constellation
Of patches and of pitches,
Not in a single world,
In things said well in music,
On the piano, and in speech,
As in a page of poetry—
Thinkers without final thoughts
In an always incipient cosmos,
The way, when we climb a mountain,
Vermont throws itself together.

A Winter Ship

BY *Sylvia Plath*

At this wharf there are no grand landings to speak of.
Red and orange barges list and blister
Shackled to the dock, outmoded, gaudy,
And apparently indestructible.
The sea pulses under a skin of oil.

A gull holds his pose on a shanty ridgepole,
Riding the tide of the wind, steady
As wood and formal, in a jacket of ashes,
The whole flat harbor anchored in
The round of his yellow eye-button.

A blimp swims up like a day-moon or tin
Cigar over his rink of fishes.
The prospect is dull as an old etching.
They are unloading three barrels of little crabs.
The pier pilings seem about to collapse

And with them that rickety edifice
Of warehouses, derricks, smokestacks, and bridges
In the distance. All around us the water slips
And gossips in its loose vernacular,
Ferrying the smells of dead cod and tar.

Farther out, the waves will be mouthing icecakes—
A poor month for park sleepers and lovers.
Even our shadows are blue with cold.
We wanted to see the sun come up
And are met, instead, by this ice-ribbed ship,

Bearded and blown, an albatross of frost,
Relic of tough weather, every winch and stay
Encased in a glassy pellicle.
The sun will diminish it soon enough:
Each wave tip glitters like a knife.

Fighting for Roses

BY *Muriel Rukeyser*

After the last freeze, in easy air,
Once the danger is past, we cut them back severely;
Pruning the weakest hardest, pruning for size
Of flower, we deprived will not deprive the sturdy.
The new shoots are preserved, the future bush
Cut down to a couple of young dormant buds.

But the early sun of April does not burn our lives:
Light straight and fiery brings back the enemies.
Claw, jaw, and crawler, all those that devour.
We work with smoke against the robber blights,
With copper against rust; the season fights itself
In deep strong rich loam under swarm attacks.

Head hidden from the wind, the power of form
Rises among these brightnesses, thorned and blowing.
Where they glow on the earth, water-drops tremble on them.
Soon we must cut them back, against damage of storms.
But those days gave us flower budded on flower,
A moment of light achieved, deep in the air of roses.

January 25th

BY *Maxine Kumin*

All night in the flue like a trapped thing,
like a broken bird,
the wind knocked unanswered.
Snow fell down the chimney, making
the forked logs spit
ashes of resurrected crickets.
By 3 A.M. both stoves were dead.
A ball of steel wool
froze to the kitchen windowsill,
while we lay back to back in bed,

two thin survivors. Somewhere in a small dream
a chipmunk uncorked from his hole
and dodged along the wall.
My love, we live at such extremes
that when, in the leftover spite of the storm,
we touch and grow warm,
I can believe I saw
the ground release
that brown and orange commonplace
sign of thaw.

Now daylight the color of buttermilk
tunnels through the coated glass.
Lie still; lie close.
Watch the sun pick
splinters from the window flowers.
Now under the ice, under twelve knee-deep layers
of mud in last summer's pond
the packed hearts of peepers are beating
barely, barely repeating
themselves enough to hang on.

For the Last Wolverine

BY *James Dickey*

They will soon be down

To one, but he still will be
For a little while   still will be stopping

The flakes in the air with a look,
Surrounding himself with the silence
Of whitening snarls. Let him eat
The last red meal of the condemned

To extinction, tearing the guts

From an elk. Yet that is not enough
For me. I would have him eat

The heart, and, from it, have an idea
Stream into his gnawing head
That he no longer has a thing
To lose, and so can walk

Out into the open, in the full

Pale of the sub-Arctic sun
Where a single spruce tree is dying

Higher and higher. Let him climb it
With all his meanness and strength.
Lord, we have come to the end
Of this kind of vision of heaven,

As the sky breaks open

Its fans around him and shimmers
And into its northern gates he rises

Snarling   complete   in the joy of a weasel
With an elk's horned heart in his stomach
Looking straight into the eternal
Blue, where he hauls his kind. I would have it all

My way: at the top of that tree I place

The New World's last eagle
Hunched in mangy feathers   giving

Up on the theory of flight.
Dear God of the wildness of poetry, let them mate
To the death in the rotten branches,
Let the tree sway and burst into flame

And mingle them, crackling with feathers,

In crownfire. Let something come
Of it   something gigantic   legendary

Rise beyond reason over hills
Of ice   SCREAMING   that it cannot die,
That it has come back, this time
On wings, and will spare no earthly thing:

That it will hover, made purely of northern

Lights, at dusk   and fall
On men building roads: will perch

On the moose's horn like a falcon
Riding into battle   into holy war against
Screaming railroad crews: will pull
Whole traplines like fibers from the snow

In the long-jawed night of fur trappers.

But, small, filthy, unwinged,
You will soon be crouching

Alone, with maybe some dim racial notion
Of being the last, but none of how much
Your unnoticed going will mean:
How much the timid poem needs

The mindless explosion of your rage,

The glutton's internal fire   the elk's
Heart in the belly, sprouting wings,

The pact of the "blind swallowing
Thing," with himself, to eat
The world, and not to be driven off it
Until it is gone, even if it takes

Forever. I take you as you are

And make of you what I will,
Skunk-bear, carcajou, bloodthirsty

Non-survivor.

Lord, let me die   but not die

Out.

Early December in Croton-on-Hudson

(FOR CHARLES HERTZ)

BY *Louise Glück*

Spiked sun. The Hudson's
Whittled down by ice.
I hear the bone dice
Of blown gravel clicking. Bone-
pale, the recent snow
Fastens like fur to the river.
Standstill. We were trying to deliver
Christmas presents when the tire blew
Last year. About the stalled Ford pines pared
Down by a storm stood, limbs bared . . .
I want you.

April

BY *Charles Wright*

The plum tree breaks out in bees.
A gull is locked like a ghost in the blue attic of heaven.
The wind goes nattering on,
Gossipy, ill at ease, in the damp rooms it will air.
I count off the grace and stays
My life has come to, and know I want less—

Divested of everything,
A downfall of light in the pine woods, motes in the rush,
Gold leaf through the undergrowth, and come back
As another name, water
Pooled in the black leaves and holding me there, to be
Released as a glint, as a flash, as a spark . . .

On the Disadvantages of Central Heating

BY *Amy Clampitt*

cold nights on the farm, a sock-shod
stove-warmed flatiron slid under
bedcovers, mornings a damascene-
sealed bizarrerie of fernwork
            decades ago now

waking in northwest London, tea
brought up steaming, a Peek Frean
biscuit alongside to be nibbled
as blue gas leaps up singing
            decades ago now

damp sheets in Dorset, fog-hung
habitat of bronchitis, of long
hot soaks in the bathtub, of nothing
quite drying out till next summer:
            delicious to think of

hassocks pulled in close, toasting-
forks held to coal-glow, strong-minded
small boys and big eager sheepdogs
muscling in on bookish profundities
now quite forgotten

the farmhouse long sold, old friends
dead or lost track of, what's salvaged
is this vivid diminuendo, unfogged
by mere affect, the perishing residue
of pure sensation

Night Blooming Cereus

BY *Katha Pollitt*

In the vacant lot behind the hospital
where rainbeaten trash, smashed bottles, gutted bedsprings
sprawl in a flyblown drowse among cinders and slag

how suddenly
dusk takes on strangeness that is more
than blue air and the blue

transient aspect of things.
Look at the ground now, how it pales and glows
as one by one, night wakers—

catchfly, dame's violet, evening lychnis—
petal by petal unfold their secret hearts
and lift to the moon a whiteness like the moon.

Why does such candor move me
more than these failed acres?
I have cherished my refusals,

I have loved them
as if they were love. I stand,
as in the nineteenth-century photograph

the women of the house, four generations
in formal black as for a great reception,
stood breathless, hushed in the shadowy conservatory

while under its glass dome
the Night Blooming Cereus
strained its whole being to an inward rhythm

stiffened its thick stalk
and pulsed out its one flower
huge, fleshy, heavy-scented, glowing, green . . .

and later little Alice Emmeline
was carried upstairs by her father, half asleep,
not understanding what it was she'd seen
but trusting it, a mystery that would keep.

Chord

BY *W. S. Merwin*

While Keats wrote they were cutting down the sandalwood forests
while he listened to the nightingale they heard their own axes echoing
through the trees
while he sat in the walled garden on the hill outside the city they
thought of their gardens dying far away on the mountain
while the sound of the words clawed at him they thought of their wives
while the tip of his pen moved the iron they had coveted was hateful to
them
while he thought of the Grecian woods they bled under red flowers
while he dreamed of wine the trees were falling from the trees
while he felt his heart they were hungry and their faith was sick
while the song broke over him they were in a secret place and they
were cutting it forever
while he coughed they carried the trunks to the hole in the forest the
size of a foreign ship
while he travelled to Italy they fell on the trails and were broken
when he lay with the odes behind him the wood was sold for cannons
when he lay watching the window they came home and lay down
and an age arrived when everything was explained in another language

The Last Night in Mithymna

BY *Linda Gregg*

Wind heaving in the trees.
My room quiet and warm.
Me on a thin mattress
looking at the full moon.
The sky black around her face.
The trees a different black
beneath. Content at last
with this world that matches
my life inside and out.
Heave and renewed heave
inside and out,
and the gentleness.
Lying alone in a cotton slip
at ten of the night in July
and a bare bulb hanging down
turned on. My bare feet
warm where they cross
at the ankle.
The cloth over the broken window
swells and goes flat
and swells again.

In Answer to Amy's Question What's a Pickerel

BY *Stanley Plumly*

Pickerel have infinite, small bones, and skins
of glass and black ground glass, and though small for pike
are no less wall-eyed and their eyes like bone.
Are fierce for their size, and when they flare
at the surface resemble drowning birds,
the wing-slick panic of birds, but in those
seconds out of water on the line,
when their color changes and they choose for life,
will try to cut you and take part of your hand
back with them. And yet they open like hands,
the sweet white meat more delicate in oil,
to be eaten off the fire when the sun
is level with the lake, the wind calm,
the air ice-blue, blue-black, and flecked with rain.

Song

BY *Rosanna Warren*

A yellow coverlet
in the greenwood:
spread the corners wide to the dim, stoop-shouldered pines.
Let blank sky
be your canopy.
Fringe the bedspread with the wall of lapsing stones.
Here faith has cut
in upright granite
"Meet me in Heaven" at the grave of each child
lost the same year,
three, buried here
a century ago. Roots and mosses hold
in the same bed
mother, daughter, dead
together, in one day. "Lord, remember the poor"
their crumbling letters pray.
I turn away.
I shall meet you nowhere, in no transfigured hour.

On soft, matted soil
blueberry bushes crawl,
each separate berry a small, hot globe of tinctured sun.
Crushed on the tongue
it releases a pang
of flesh. Tender flesh, slipped from its skin,
preserves its blue heat
down my throat.

What I Did on a Rainy Day

BY *May Swenson*

Breathed the fog from the valley
Inhaled its ether fumes
With whittling eyes peeled the hills
to their own blue and bone
Swallowed piercing pellets of rain
caught cloudsful in one colorless cup
Exhaling stung the earth with sunlight
struck leaf and bristle to green fire
Turned tree trunks to gleaming pillars
and twigs to golden nails
With one breath taken into the coils
of my blood and given again when vibrant
I showed who's god around here

Mockingbirds

BY *Mary Oliver*

This morning
two mockingbirds
in the green field
were spinning and tossing

the white ribbons
of their songs
into the air.
I had nothing

better to do
than listen.
I mean this
seriously.

In Greece,
a long time ago,
an old couple
opened their door

to two strangers
who were,
it soon appeared,
not men at all,

but gods.
It is my favorite story—
how the old couple
had almost nothing to give

but their willingness
to be attentive—
but for this alone
the gods loved them

and blessed them—
when they rose
out of their mortal bodies,
like a million particles of water

from a fountain,
the light
swept into all the corners
of the cottage,

and the old couple,
shaken with understanding,
bowed down—
but still they asked for nothing

but the difficult life
which they had already.
And the gods smiled, as they vanished,
clapping their great wings.

Wherever it was
I was supposed to be
this morning—
whatever it was I said

I would be doing—
I was standing
at the edge of the field—
I was hurrying

through my own soul,
opening its dark doors—
I was leaning out;
I was listening.

Dooryard Flower

BY *Ellen Bryant Voigt*

Because you're sick I want to bring you flowers—
unforced, neither imported nor potted,
flowers from the landscape that you love—
because it is your birthday and you're sick
I want to bring outdoors inside,
the natural and wild, picked by my hand,
but nothing is blooming here but daffodils,
archipelagic in the short green
early grass, erupted
bulbs planted decades before we came,
the edge of where a garden once was kept
extended now in a string of islands I straddle
as in a fairy tale, harvesting,
not taking the single blossom from a clump
but thinning where they're thickest, tall-stemmed
from the mother patch, dwarf to the west, most
fully opened in a blowsy whorl,
one with a pale spider luffing her thread,
one with a slow beetle chewing the lip, a few
with what seems almost a lion's face, a lion's mane,
and because there is a shadow on your lungs, your liver,
and elsewhere, hidden,

some of those with delicate green
streaks in the clown's ruff (corolla—
actually made from adapted leaves), and more
right this moment starting to unfold, I've gathered
my two fists full, I carry them like a bride,
I am bringing you the only glorious thing
in the yards and fields between my house and yours,
none of the tulips budded yet, the lilac
a sheaf of sticks, the apple trees
withheld, the birch unleaved—
it could still be winter here, were it not
for green dotted with gold, but you won't wait
for dogtoothed violets, trillium under the pines,
and who could bear azaleas, dogwood, early profuse rose
of somewhere else when you are assaulted here, early May,
not any calm narcissus, orange corona
on scalloped white, not even its slender stalk
in a fountain of leaves, no stiff cornets of the honest
jonquils, gendered parts upthrust in brass and cream:
just this common flash in anyone's yard,
scrambled cluster of petals
crayon-yellow, as in a child's drawing of the sun,
I'm bringing you a sun, a children's choir, host
of transient voices—wasn't it always
anyone's child you loved?—first bright
splash in the gray exhausted world, a feast
of the dooryard flower we call butter-and-egg.

For the Lichens

BY *Jane Hirshfield*

Back then, what did I know?
The names of subway lines, buses.
How long it took to walk twenty blocks.

Uptown and downtown.
Not north, not south, not you.

When I saw you, later, seaweed reefed in the air,
you were gray-green, incomprehensible, old.
What you clung to, hung from: old.
Trees looking half dead, stones.

Marriage of fungi and algae,
chemists of air,
changers of nitrogen-unusable into nitrogen-usable.

Like those nameless ones
who kept painting, shaping, engraving
unseen, unread, unremembered.
Not caring if they were no good, if they were past it.

Rock wools, water fans, earth scale, mouse ears, dust,
ash-of-the-woods.
Transformers unvalued, uncounted.
Cell by cell, word by word, making a world they could live in.

I Stare at a Cormorant

BY *Tiana Clark*

with its waterlogged wings spread open,
drying off on a rock in the middle
of a man-made lake after diving for food
and it makes me think about wonder
and it makes me want to pry and stretch
my shy arms open to the subtle summer
wind slicing through the park, sliding
over my skin like a stream of people
blowing candles out over my feathery
body and it makes me think about my
church when I was a kid, and how I
lifted my hands to Jesus, hoping
for surrender, but often felt nothing,
except for the rush of fervent people wanting
to be delivered from their aching, present
pain, and how that ache changed the smell
in the room to money and how I pinched
my face and especially my eyes tighter,
tighter and reached my hands higher—how
I, like the cormorant, stood in the middle
of the sanctuary so exposed and open
and wanted and wanted so much to grasp

the electric weather rushing through
the drama of it all like a shout
in the believer's scratchy throat.

I don't go to church anymore, but today
I woke up early and meditated. I closed
my eyes and focused on a fake seed
in my hand and put my hands over
my heart to shove the intention inside
my chest to blossom—I'm still stumbling
through this life hoping for anyone or
something to save me. I'm still thinking
about the cormorant who disappeared
when I was writing this poem. I was just
looking down and finishing a line
and then I looked back up—gone.

Hotel Earth

BY *James Longenbach*

Cornices overgrown with moss, the stoop
With nettles, flower beds
Hardly discernible beneath brambles and weeds—

Next door was a place where drinks
Were sold, so I ordered
A glass of red wine. *The Earth?*

For years it never changed, said the bartender.
Now kids won't come around at night.
Doors close by themselves

As if clouds were gathering—bang!
Footsteps climb the staircase, one, two—
I paid the tab. Does anything stay

There—hatred, the capacity for love?
There's the baby in the red striped sweater
Against blue sky, my left hand

Holding her, my right the camera.
She's smiling at you.
We're invisible, like the sea.

The Origin Revisited

BY *Ada Limón*

— After a visit to the Yaak Valley in Kootenai National Forest, Montana, where the U.S. Forest Service had announced a logging project called Black Ram

What is there to be done now, but enter
          against abandonment, become a hollow sound

in the halo of labyrinthine green, become a crossed-
          out word on the back of someone's hand.

Once, all of this became

          all of this. One not-yet-golden western larch
curves by a white pine, a white pine

          curves by a western hemlock, no one here
is heroic. To enter here is to enter

magnitude, to feel an ecstatic somethingness,
          a nothingness of your own name.

All words become wrong. A whole world exists
          without us. But who is us?

Lichen, moss, grizzly scat, moose hoofprint like two
exclamation points by the drying frog pond.

How do you know you're alive? What evidence
will you leave? So many myths

are unraveling; a yellow swallowtail glides by over
the sinless creek bed. A storm

wets the skin and we are surprised we have
skin. Woods' rose, white-flowered rhododendron,

nothing here is unfinished. What it gave me? I saw
a new tree emerge out of a ground made of ancient trees

on top of more ancient trees, on top of more ancient trees,
on top of more ancient trees, and understood then

that this was how the Earth was made.

Two Apricots

BY *Ama Codjoe*

In Kadıköy market, their money already
mingled, someone fished for coins
and handed a small few to the grocer; the other
inspected the apricots and kept the one
less beautiful. Each revealed, at their fingertips,
a pink moon. The firmament tasted like
an insatiable kiss. They held each other's hands—
dirty from money, sticky with juice.

III.

PERSONAL MYTHOLOGIES

Days

BY *Ralph Waldo Emerson*

Daughters of Time, the hypocritic Days,
Muffled and dumb, like barefoot dervishes,
And marching single in an endless file,
Bring diadems and fagots in their hands.
To each they offer gifts, after his will,—
Bread, kingdoms, stars, or sky that holds them all.
I, in my pleached garden, watched the pomp,
Forgot my morning wishes, hastily
Took a few herbs and apples, and the Day
Turned and departed silent. I, too late,
Under her solemn fillet saw the scorn.

Bardic Symbols

BY *Walt Whitman*

I.

Elemental drifts!
Oh, I wish I could impress others as you and the waves have just been impressing me!

II.

As I ebbed with an ebb of the ocean of life,
As I wended the shores I know,
As I walked where the sea-ripples wash you, Paumanok,
Where they rustle up, hoarse and sibilant,
Where the fierce old mother endlessly cries for her castaways,
I, musing, late in the autumn day, gazing off southward,
Alone, held by the eternal self of me that threatens to get the better of me and stifle me,
Was seized by the spirit that trails in the lines underfoot,
In the ruin, the sediment, that stands for all the water and all the land of the globe.

III.

Fascinated, my eyes, reverting from the south, dropped, to follow those
  slender windrows,
Chaff, straw, splinters of wood, weeds, and the sea-gluten,
Scum, scales from shining rocks, leaves of salt-lettuce, left by the tide.

IV.

Miles walking, the sound of breaking waves the other side of me,
Paumanok, there and then as I thought the old thought of likenesses,
These you presented to me, you fish-shaped island,
As I wended the shores I know,
As I walked with that eternal self of me, seeking types.

V.

As I wend the shores I know not,
As I listen to the dirge, the voices of men and women wrecked,
As I inhale the impalpable breezes that set in upon me,
As the ocean so mysterious rolls toward me closer and closer,
At once I find, the least thing that belongs to me, or that I see or touch,
  I know not;
I, too, but signify a little washed-up drift,—a few sands and dead leaves
  to gather,
Gather, and merge myself as part of the leaves and drift.

VI.

Oh, baffled, lost,
Bent to the very earth, here preceding what follows,
Terrified with myself that I have dared to open my mouth,
Aware now, that, amid all the blab whose echoes recoil upon me,
    I have not once had the least idea who or what I am,
But that before all my insolent poems the real me still stands
    untouched, untold, altogether unreached,
Withdrawn far, mocking me with mock-congratulatory signs and bows,
With peals of distant ironical laughter at every word I have written or
    shall write,
Striking me with insults, till I fall helpless upon the sand!

VII.

Oh, I think I have not understood anything,—not a single object,—
    and that no man ever can!

VIII.

I think Nature here, in sight of the sea, is taking advantage of me to
    oppress me,
Because I was assuming so much,
And because I have dared to open my mouth to sing at all.

IX.

You oceans both! You tangible land! Nature!
Be not too stern with me,—I submit,—I close with you,—
These little shreds shall, indeed, stand for all.

X.

You friable shore, with trails of debris!
You fish-shaped island! I take what is underfoot:
What is yours is mine, my father!

XI.

I, too, Paumanok,
I, too, have bubbled up, floated the measureless float, and been washed
on your shores.

XII.

I, too, am but a trail of drift and debris,—
I, too, leave little wrecks upon you, you fish-shaped island!

XIII.

I throw myself upon your breast, my father!
I cling to you so that you cannot unloose me,—
I hold you so firm, till you answer me something.

XIV.

Kiss me, my father!
Touch me with your lips, as I touch those I love!
Breathe to me, while I hold you close, the secret of the wondrous
murmuring I envy!
For I fear I shall become crazed, if I cannot emulate it, and utter myself
as well as it.

XV.

Sea-raff! Torn leaves!
Oh, I sing, some day, what you have certainly said to me!

XVI.

Ebb, ocean of life! (the flow will return,)—
Cease not your moaning, you fierce old mother!
Endlessly cry for your castaways! Yet fear not, deny not me,—
Rustle not up so hoarse and angry against my feet, as I touch you, or
gather from you.

XVII.

I mean tenderly by you,—
I gather for myself, and for this phantom, looking down where we
lead, and following me and mine.

XVIII.

Me and mine!
We, loose windrows, little corpses,
Froth, snowy white, and bubbles,
Tufts of straw, sands, fragments,
Buoyed hither from many moods, one contradicting another,
From the storm, the long calm, the darkness, the swell,
Musing, pondering, a breath, a briny tear, a dab of liquid or soil,
Up just as much out of fathomless workings fermented and thrown,
A limp blossom or two, torn, just as much over waves floating, drifted
at random,

Just as much for us that sobbing dirge of Nature,
Just as much, whence we come, that blare of the cloud-trumpets,—
We, capricious, brought hither, we know not whence, spread out before
you,—you, up there, walking or sitting,
Whoever you are,—we, too, lie in drifts at your feet.

After the Burial

BY *James Russell Lowell*

Yes, Faith is a goodly anchor;
   When skies are sweet as a psalm,
At the bows it lolls so stalwart
   In bluff broad-shouldered calm.

And when, over breakers to leeward
   The tattered surges are hurled,
It may keep our head to the tempest,
   With its grip on the base of the world.

But, after the shipwreck, tell me
   What help in its iron thews,
Still true to the broken hawser,
   Deep down among sea-weed and ooze?

In the breaking gulfs of sorrow,
   When the helpless feet stretch out,
And find in the deeps of darkness
   No footing so solid as doubt,

Then better one spar of memory,
   One broken plank of the past,
That our human heart may cling to,
   Though hopeless of shore at last!

To the spirit its splendid conjectures,
   To the flesh its sweet despair,
Its tears o'er the thin-worn locket
   With its beauty of deathless hair!

Immortal? I feel it and know it;
   Who doubts it of such as she?
But that is the pang's very secret,—
   Immortal away from me!

There's a narrow ridge in the graveyard
   Would scarce stay a child in his race;
But to me and my thought it is wider
   Than the star-sown vague of space.

Your logic, my friend, is perfect,
   Your morals most drearily true,
But the earth that stops my darling's ears
   Makes mine insensate too.

Console, if you will; I can bear it;
  'Tis a well-meant alms of breath;
But not all the preaching since Adam
  Has made Death other than Death.

Communion in spirit! Forgive me,
  But I, who am earthy and weak,
Would give all my incomes from dreamland
  For her rose-leaf palm on my cheek!

That little shoe in the corner,
  So worn and wrinkled and brown,—
Its motionless hollow confutes you,
  And argues your wisdom down.

Flammantia Mœnia Mundi

BY *Annie Fields*

I stood alone in purple space, and saw
The burning walls of the world like wings of flame
Circling the sphere. There was no break nor flaw
In those great fiery battlements, whence came
The spirits who had done with time and fame,
And all the playthings of earth's little hour.
I saw them pass; I knew them for the same,—
Mothers and brothers and the sons of power.

Yet were they changed; the fires of death had burned
Their perishable selves, and there remained
Only the pure white vision of the soul,—
The mortal part consumed, and quick returned
Ashes to ashes; while, unscathed, unstained,
The immortal passed beyond the earth's control.

Prime

BY *Amy Lowell*

Your voice is like bells over roofs at dawn
When a bird flies
And the sky changes to a fresher color.

Speak, speak, Beloved.
Say little things
For my ears to catch
And run with them to my heart.

Come In

BY *Robert Frost*

As I came to the edge of the woods,
Thrush music—hark!
Now if it was dusk outside,
Inside it was dark.

Too dark in the woods for a bird
By sleight of wing
To better its perch for the night,
Though it still could sing.

The last of the light of the sun
That had died in the west
Still lived for one song more
In a thrush's breast.

Far in the pillared dark
Thrush music went—
Almost like a call to come in
To the dark and lament.

But no, I was out for stars:
I would not come in.
I meant not even if asked;
And I hadn't been.

Ideal Landscape

BY *Adrienne Rich*

We had to take the world as it was given:
The nursemaid sitting passive in the park
Was rarely by a changeling prince accosted.
The mornings happened similar and stark
In rooms of selfhood where we woke and lay
Watching today unfold like yesterday.

Our friends were not unearthly beautiful,
Nor spoke with tongues of gold; our lovers blundered
Now and again when most we sought perfection,
Or hid in cupboards when the heavens thundered.
The human rose to haunt us everywhere,
Raw, flawed, and asking more than we could bear.

And always time was rushing like a tram
Through streets of a foreign city, streets we saw
Opening into great and sunny squares
We could not find again, no map could show—
Never those fountains tossed in that same light,
Those gilded trees, those statues green and white.

Circle of Breath

BY *William Stafford*

The night my father died the moon shone on the snow.
I drove in from the west; Mother was at the door.
All the light in the room extended like a shadow.
Truant from knowing, I stood where the great dark fell.

There was a time before, something we used to tell—
how we parked the car in a storm and walked into a field
to know how it was to be cut off, out in the dark alone.
My father and I stood together while the storm went by.

A windmill was there in the field giving its little cry
while we stood calm in ourselves, knowing we could go home.
But I stood on the skull of the world the night he died, and knew
that I leased a place to live with my white breath.

Truant no more, I stepped forward and learned his death.

Eleutheria

BY *James Wright*

Rubbing her mouth along my mouth, she lost
Illusions of the sky, the dreams it offered:
The pale cloud walking home to winter, dust
Blown to a shell of sails so far above
That autumn landscape where we lay and suffered
The fruits of summer in the fields of love.

We lay and heard the apples fall for hours,
The stripping twilight plundered trees of boughs,
The land dissolved beneath the rabbit's heels,
And far away I heard a window close,
A haying wagon heave and catch its wheels,
Some water slide and stumble and be still.
The dark began to climb the empty hill.

If dark Eleutheria turned and lay
Forever beside me, who would care for years?
The throat, the supple belly, the warm thigh
Burgeoned against the earth; I lay afraid,
For who could bear such beauty under the sky?

I would have held her loveliness in air,
Away from things that lured me to decay:
The ground's deliberate riches, fallen pears,
Bewildered apples blown to mounds of shade.

Lovers' location is the first to fade.
They wander back in winter, but there is
No comfortable grass to couch a dress.
Musicians of the yellow weeds are dead.
And she, remembering something, turns to hear
Either a milkweed float or a thistle fall.
Bodiless shadow thrown along a wall,
She glides lightly; the pale year follows her.

The moments ride away, the locust flute
Is silvered thin and lost, over and over.
She will return some evening to discover
The tree uplifted to the very root,
The leaves shouldered away, with lichen grown
Among the interlacings of the stone,
October blowing dust, and summer gone
Into a dark barn, like a hiding lover.

Anxiety

BY *A. K. Ramanujan*

Not branchless as the fear tree
it has naked roots and secret twigs.
Not geometric as the parabolas
of hope, it has loose ends
with a knot at the top
that's me.
                    Not wakeful in its white-snake
glassy ways like the eloping gaiety of waters,
it drowses, viscous and fibered as pitch.

Flames have only lungs. Water is all eyes.
The earth has bone for muscle. And the air
is a flock of invisible pigeons.
                                                            But anxiety
can find no metaphor to end it.

The Lost Pilot

FOR MY FATHER, 1922–1944

BY *James Tate*

Your face did not rot
like the other—the co-pilot,
for example, I saw him

yesterday. His face is corn-
mush: his wife and daughter,
the poor ignorant people, stare

as if he will compose soon.
He was more wronged than Job.
But your face did not rot

like the others—it grew dark,
and hard like ebony;
the features progressed in their

distinction. If I could cajole
you to come back for an evening,
down from your compulsive

orbiting, I would touch you,
read your face as Dallas,
your hoodlum gunner, now,

with the blistered eyes, reads
his braille editions. I would
touch your face as a disinterested

scholar touches an original page.
However frightening, I would
discover you, and I would not

turn you in; I would not make
you face your wife, or Dallas,
or the co-pilot, Jim. You

could return to your crazy
orbiting, and I would not try
to fully understand what

it means to you. All I know
is this: when I see you,
as I have seen you at least

once every year of my life,
spin across the wilds of the sky
like a tiny, African god,

I feel dead. I feel as if I were
the residue of a stranger's life,
that I should pursue you.

My head cocked toward the sky,
I cannot get off the ground,
and, you, passing over again,

fast, perfect, and unwilling
to tell me that you are doing
well, or that it was mistake

that placed you in that world,
and me in this; or that misfortune
placed these worlds in us.

Last Words

BY *James Merrill*

My life, your light green eyes
Have lit on me with joy.
There's nothing I don't know
Or shall not know again,
Over and over again.
It's noon. It's dawn. It's night.
I am the dog that dies
In the deep street of Troy.
Tomorrow. Long ago.
Part of me dims with pain,
Becomes the stinging flies,
The bent head of the boy.
Part looks into your light
And lives to tell you so.

Girl and Horse, 1928

BY *Margaret Atwood*

You are younger than I am, you are
someone I never knew, you stand
under a tree, your face half-shadowed,
holding the horse by its bridle.

Why do you smile? Can't you
see the apple blossoms falling around
you, snow, sun, snow, listen, the tree
dries and is being burnt, the wind

is bending your body, your face
ripples like water   where did you go
But no, you stand there exactly
the same, you can't hear me, forty

years ago you were caught by light
and fixed in that secret
place where we live, where we believe
nothing can change, grow older.

(On the other side
of the picture, the instant
is over, the shadow
of the tree has moved. You wave,

then turn and ride
out of sight through the vanished
orchard, still smiling
as though you do not notice)

The Ghosts

BY *Kathryn Ungerer*

From the field she calls John, John. O
remember then the quick fall
of daylight on her dress, the field
sprigged with blue-eyed grasses.
It is the first morning of the world. Only
here among the bloodroot, under
the thick, white flowers, he sees the sun
pick at a rabbit, left behind
by winter. Memory replaces
worship. And she watches

his thigh pressed to the stove,
the implacable spread of frost
on the windowpane. It is night. The babies
are all gone. Humming she hears the first
star's tentative, hungry words. He has been
held there for years. The moon
has washed his face of all blood.

The Name of the Air

BY *Philip Levine*

They would arrive late
because of the rumor of war
and move slowly, fearing
the Lord in a Whirlwind
who hovered always above
U.S. 24. They ate
everything and drank steadily
and were never drunk.
The gifts they left
weren't here in the morning
nor were they, who left
somewhere near the end
when the cake collapsed,
the rug smoldered,
and the dances choked. They
are here in my hand, faceless
in the sudden flash, bowing
to sunlight or turning in a smear
of shade, thumbprints
on an oily knife, and so pass
to the future to breathe
only when I breathe and lightly

not to distress the smoke
and stain the brow of
the woman in white and the man
in black, holding hands,
who turn suddenly away
from each other to stare
into the twin eyes of darkness
or read this first time
the name of the air.

Heroic Simile

BY *Robert Hass*

When the swordsman fell in Kurosawa's *Seven Samurai*
in the gray rain,
in Cinemascope and the Tokugawa dynasty,
he fell straight as a pine, he fell
as Ajax fell in Homer
in chanted dactyls and the tree was so huge
the woodsman returned for two days
to that lucky place before he was done with the sawing
and on the third day he brought his uncle.

They stacked logs in the resinous air,
hacking the small limbs off,
tying those bundles separately.
The slabs near the root
were quartered and still they were awkwardly large.
The logs from midtree they halved:
ten bundles and four great piles of fragrant wood,
moons and quarter moons and half moons
ridged by the saw's tooth.

The woodsman and the old man his uncle
are standing in midforest

on a floor of pine silt and spring mud.
They have stopped working
because they are tired and because
I have imagined no pack animal
or primitive wagon. They are too canny
to call in neighbors and come home
with a few logs after three days' work.
They are waiting for me to do something
or for the overseer of the Great Lord
to come and arrest them.

How patient they are!
The old man smokes a pipe and spits.
The young man is thinking he would be rich
if he were already rich and had a mule.
Ten days of hauling
and on the seventh day they'll probably
be caught, go home empty-handed
or worse. I don't know
whether they're Japanese or Mycenaean
and there's nothing I can do.
The path from here to that village
is not translated. A hero, dying,
gives off stillness to the air.
A man and a woman walk from the movies
to the house in the silence of separate fidelities.
There are limits to imagination.

Monarchs

BY *Sharon Olds*

All morning as I sit thinking of you
the Monarchs are passing. Seven stories up,
to the left of the river, they are making their way
south, their wings the dark red of your
hands like butchers' hands, the raised
veins of their wings like your scars.
I could scarcely feel your massive rough
palms on me, your touch was so light,
the delicate chapped scrape of an insect's leg
across my breast. No one had ever
touched me before. I didn't know enough to
open my legs, but felt your thighs,
feathered with red-gold hairs
          opening
between my legs like a
pair of wings.

The hinged print of my blood on your thighs—
a winged creature pinned there—
and then you left, as you were to leave
over and over, the butterflies moving
in masses past my window, floating
south to their transformation, crossing over
borders in the night, the diffuse blood-red
cloud of them, my body under yours,
the beauty and silence of the great migrations.

Sudden Journey

BY *Tess Gallagher*

Maybe I'm seven in the open field—
the straw-grass so high
only the top of my head makes a curve
of brown in the yellow. Rain then.
First a little. A few drops on my
wrist, the right wrist. More rain.
My shoulders, my chin. Until I'm looking up
to let my eyes take the bliss.
I open my face. Let the teeth show. I
pull my shirt down past the collar-bones.
I'm still a boy under my breast spots.
I can drink anywhere. The rain. My
skin shattering. Up suddenly, needing
to gulp, turning with my tongue, my arms out
running, running in the hard, cold plenitude
of all those who reach earth by falling.

A Visitor

BY *Mary Oliver*

My father, for example,
who was young once
and blue-eyed,
returns
on the darkest of nights
to the porch and knocks
wildly at the door,
and if I answer
I must be prepared
for his waxy face,
for his lower lip
swollen with bitterness.
And so, for a long time,
I did not answer,
but slept fitfully
between his hours of rapping.
But finally there came the night
when I rose out of my sheets
and stumbled down the hall.
The door fell open

and I knew I was saved
and could bear him,
pathetic and hollow,
with even the least of his dreams
frozen inside him,
and the meanness gone.
And I greeted him and asked him
into the house,
and lit the lamp,
and looked into his blank eyes
in which at last
I saw what a child must love,
I saw what love might have done
had we loved in time.

The Wide and Varied World

Women, women, what do they want?

BY *Ellen Bryant Voigt*

The first ones in the door of the plant-filled office
were the twins, fresh from the upper grades,
their matched coats dangling open.
And then their more compliant brother, leading
the dear stuffed tottering creature—amazing
that she could lift her leg high enough
to cross the threshold to the waiting-room.
Then the woman, the patient, carrying the baby
in an infant seat, his every inch of flesh
swaddled against the vicious weather.
Once inside, how skillfully the mother
unwound the many layers—
                                        and now so quickly
must restore them: news from the lab
has passed through the nurse's sliding window.
The youngest, strapped again into his shell,
fusses for the breast, the twins tease their sister,
the eight-year-old looks almost wise as his mother
struggles into her coat with one hand and with the other
pinches his sweaty neck, her hissed threats
swarming his face like flies.

Now she's gone.
The women remaining don't need to speak.
Outside, snow falls in the streets
and quiet hills, and seems, in the window,
framed by the room's continuous greenery,
to obliterate the wide and varied world.
We half-smile, half-nod to one another.
One returns to her magazine.
One shifts gently to the right arm
her sleeping newborn, unfurls the bud of its hand.
One of us takes her turn in the inner office
where she submits to the steel table
and removes from her body its stubborn wish.
We want what you want, only
we have to want it more.

Execution

BY *Edward Hirsch*

The last time I saw my high school football coach
He had cancer stenciled into his face
Like pencil marks from the sun, like intricate
Drawings on the chalkboard, small *x*'s and *o*'s
That he copied down in a neat numerical hand
Before practice in the morning. By day's end
The board was a spiderweb of options and counters,
Blasts and sweeps, a constellation of players
Shining under his favorite word, *Execution*,
Underlined in the upper right-hand corner of things.
He believed in football like a new religion
And had perfect, unquestioning faith in the fundamentals
Of blocking and tackling, the idea of warfare
Without suffering or death, the concept of teammates
Moving in harmony like the planets—and yet
Our awkward adolescent bodies were always canceling
The flawless beauty of Saturday afternoons in September,
Falling away from the particular grace of autumn,
The clear weather, the ideal game he imagined.

And so he drove us through punishing drills
On weekday afternoons, and doubled our practice time,
And challenged us to hammer him with forearms,
And devised elaborate, last-second plays—a flea-
Flicker, a triple reverse—to save us from defeat.
Almost always they worked. He despised losing
And loved winning more than his own body, maybe even
More than himself. But the last time I saw him
He looked wobbly and stunned by illness,
And I remembered the game in my senior year
When we met a downstate team who loved hitting
More than we did, who battered us all afternoon
With a vengeance, who destroyed us with timing
And power, with deadly, impersonal authority,
Machine-like fury, perfect execution.

Late Loving

BY *Mona Van Duyn*

"What Christ was saying, what he meant [in the story of Mary and Martha] was that the pleasures of that hair, that ointment, must be taken. Because the accidents of death would deprive us soon enough. We must not deprive ourselves, our loved ones, of the luxury of our extravagant affections. We must not try to second-guess death by refusing to love the ones we loved. . . . "

—Mary Gordon, *Final Payments*

If in my mind I marry you every year
it is to calm an extravagance of love
with dousing custom, for it flames up fierce
and wild whenever I forget that we live
in double rooms whose temperature's controlled
by matrimony's turned-down thermostat.
I need the mnemonics, now that we are old,
of oath and law in re-memorizing that.
Our dogs are dead, our child never came true.
I might use up, in my weak-mindedness,
the whole human supply of warmth on you
before I could think of others and digress.
"Love" is finding the familiar dear.
"In love" is to be taken by surprise.

Over, in the shifty face you wear,
and over, in the assessments of your eyes,
you change, and with new sweet or barbed word
find out new entrances to my inmost nerve.
When you stand at the stove it's I who am most stirred.
When you finish work I rest without reserve.
Daytimes, sometimes, our three-legged race seems slow.
Squabbling onward, we chafe from being so near.
But all night long we lie like crescents of Velcro,
turning together till we re-adhere.
Since you, with longer stride and better vision,
more clearly see the finish line, I stoke
my hurrying self, to keep it in condition,
with light and life-renouncing meals of smoke.
As when a collector scoops two Monarchs in
at once, whose fresh flights to and from each other
are netted down, so in vows I re-imagine
I re-invoke what keeps us stale together.
What you try to give is more than I want to receive,
yet each month when you pick up scissors for our appointment
and my cut hair falls and covers your feet I believe
that the house is filled again with the odor of ointment.

The Bad Physician

BY *Linda Gregerson*

The body in health, the body in sickness,
                    inscribing
          its versatile logic till the least

of us must, willy nilly, learn
                    to read.
          And even in error, as when

the mutant multiplies, or first
                    my right eye,
          now my left, is targeted

for harm by the system
                    designed
          to keep it safe—

even in error the body
                    wields cunning
          as birches in leaf wield light.

The child who swallows the amnion now
                    will swallow milk
          by winter. The milk

can find a use for me but not
for my belief,
nor yours, and it beggars the best

of our purposes. Within us
without us,
this life is already beyond us,

so what must it make of the man who cures
by rote?
My friend's young daughter moved

with a slightly muddied
gait,
and then her tongue

and then her hands
unlearned
their freedom, so newly

acquired. Unlearned with great
labor
while the tumor thrived,

and all the elixirs in Mexico
could not
revise her sentence by a day.

You who make your living at
the body's re-
versible deviations,

what will you say to a six-
year-old
when all her bright first lessons

are defaced? Even the skeptic
in his lab,
who works at the friable boundaries

of our common
legibility
and does the work that I trust

best, is bound to frame his question
in the pure,
distorting light of hope.

The beautiful cells dividing have
no mind
for us, but look

what a ravishing mind
they make
and what a heart we've nursed

in its shade, who love
                    that most
            which leaves us most behind.

Emptiness

BY *Kay Ryan*

Emptiness cannot be
compressed. Nor can it
fight abuse. Nor is there
an endless West hosting
elk, antelope, and the
tough cayuse. This is
true also of the mind:
it can get used.

What the Living Do

BY *Marie Howe*

Johnny, the kitchen sink has been clogged for days, some utensil
probably fell down there.
And the Drāno won't work but smells dangerous, and the crusty dishes
have piled up

waiting for the plumber I still haven't called. This is the everyday we
spoke of.
It's winter again: the sky's a deep, headstrong blue, and the sunlight
pours through

the open living-room windows because the heat's on too high in here
and I can't turn it off.
For weeks now, driving, or dropping a bag of groceries in the street,
the bag breaking,

I've been thinking: This is what the living do. And yesterday, hurrying
along those
wobbly bricks in the Cambridge sidewalk, spilling my coffee down my
wrist and sleeve,

I thought it again, and again later, when buying a hairbrush: This is it.
Parking. Slamming the car door shut in the cold. What you called *that
yearning*.

What you finally gave up. We want the spring to come and the winter
to pass. We want
whoever to call or not call, a letter, a kiss—we want more and more
and then more of it.

But there are moments, walking, when I catch a glimpse of myself in
the window glass,
say, the window of the corner video store, and I'm gripped by a
cherishing so deep

for my own blowing hair, chapped face, and unbuttoned coat that I'm
speechless:
I am living. I remember you.

As from a Quiver of Arrows

BY *Carl Phillips*

What do we do with the body, do we
burn it, do we set it in dirt or in
stone, do we wrap it in balm, honey,
oil, and then gauze and tip it onto
and trust it to a raft and to water?

What will happen to the memory of his
body, if one of us doesn't hurry now
and write it down fast? Will it be
salt or late light that it melts like?
Floss, rubber gloves, a chewed cap

to a pen elsewhere—how are we to
regard his effects, do we throw them
or use them away, do we say they are
relics and so treat them like relics?
Does his soiled linen count? If so,

would we be wrong, then, to wash it?
There are no instructions whether it
should go to where are those with no

linen, or whether by night we should
memorially wear it ourselves, by day

reflect upon it folded, shelved, empty.
Here, on the floor behind his bed, is
a bent photo—why? Were the two of
them lovers? Does it mean, where we
found it, that he forgot it or lost it

or intended a safekeeping? Should we
attempt to make contact? What if this
other man too is dead? Or alive, but
doesn't want to remember, is human?
Is it okay to be human, and fall away

from oblation and memory, if we forget,
and can't sometimes help it and sometimes
it is all that we want? How long, in
dawns or new cocks, does that take?
What if it is rest and nothing else that

we want? Is it a findable thing, small?
In what hole is it hidden? Is it, maybe,
a country? Will a guide be required who
will say to us how? Do we fly? Do we
swim? What will I do now, with my hands?

Colostrum

BY *Kevin Young*

We are not born
with tears. Your

first dozen cries
are dry.

It takes some time
for the world to arrive

and salt the eyes.

Articulation

BY *Natasha Trethewey*

—After Miguel Cabrera's portrait of Saint Gertrude, 1763

In the legend, Saint Gertrude is called to write
after seeing, in a vision, the sacred heart of Christ.

Cabrera paints her among the instruments
of her faith: quill, inkwell, an open book,

rings on her fingers like Christ's many wounds—
the heart emblazoned on her chest, the holy

infant nestled there as if sunk deep in a wound.
Against the dark backdrop, her face is a wafer

of light. How not to see, in the saint's image,
my mother's last portrait—the dark backdrop,

her dress black as a habit, the bright edge
of her afro ringing her face with light? And how

not to recall her many wounds: ring finger
shattered, her ex-husband's bullet finding

her temple, lodging where her last thought lodged?
Three weeks gone, my mother came to me

in a dream, her body whole again but for
one perfect wound, the singular articulation

of all of them: a hole, center of her forehead,
the size of a wafer—light pouring from it.

How, then, could I not answer her life
with mine, she who saved me with hers?

And how could I not, bathed in the light
of her wound, find my calling there?

Ars Poetica with Mother and Dogs

BY *Rio Cortez*

I turn and don't expect my mother's face
                    I ask *how did you enter this poem*
she says it wasn't easy

she is dressed in my favorite horse-print silk sheath
                    and dripping lake water
says she wore it to trick my lover

I want to ask *how could you* but instead
                    I reach behind her and break a vase
she used to love but we are surrounded

by dogs some of them used to sleep
                    at our bedsides but don't
anymore she grabs my hand and who am I anyway

to keep asking
                    her to leave why not take her face
and explain the damned thing

There You Are

BY *Victoria Adukwei Bulley*

There you are
this cold day
boiling the water on the stove,
pouring the herbs into the pot,
hawthorn, rose;
buying the tulips
& looking at them, holding
your heart in your hands at the table
saying *please, please*, to nobody else
there in the kitchen with you.
How hard, how heavy this all is.
How beautiful, these things you do,
in case they help, these things you do
that, although you haven't said it yet,
say that you want to live.

PERMISSIONS

LITANY FOR DICTATORSHIPS by Stephen Vincent Benet, from Selected Works of Stephen Vincent Benet Holt, Rinehart and Winston, copyright © 1935 by Stephen Vincent Benet. Copyright renewed ©1963 by Thomas C. Benet, Stephanie B. Mahin, and Rachel Benet Lewis. Used by permission of Brandt & Hochman Literary Agents, Inc. All rights reserved.

"In Texas". Copyright © 1948 by May Sarton, from COLLECTED POEMS 1930-1993 by May Sarton. Used by permission of W. W. Norton & Company, Inc.

"Dark Symphony" in Harlem Gallery and Other Poems of Melvin B Tolson, Melvin B. Tolson, Jr. Edited by Raymond Nelson. Introduction by Rita Dove. pp. 35-43. © 1999 by the Rector and Visitors of the University of Virginia. Reprinted by permission of the University of Virginia Press.

Charles Olson, "Pacific Lament" from The Collected Poems of Charles Olson: Excluding the Maximus Poems. Copyright © 1997 by Charles Olson. Reprinted with the permission of Copyright Clearance Center on behalf of University of California Press.

"Frederick Douglass". Copyright © 1966 by Robert Hayden, from COLLECTED POEMS OF ROBERT HAYDEN by Robert Hayden, edited by Frederick Glaysher. Used by permission of Liveright Publishing Corporation.

"For the Union Dead" from COLLECTED POEMS by Robert Lowell. Copyright © 2003 by Harriet Lowell and Sheridan Lowell. Reprinted by permission of Farrar, Straus and Giroux. All Rights Reserved.

"A Good View from Flagstaff," originally printed in "White Center" poems by Richard Hugo (1980) but also available and in print "Making Certain It Goes On" the collected poems of Richard Hugo (1984).

"Welcome to Hiroshima" from HENRY PURCELL IN JAPAN by Mary Jo Salter, copyright © 1984 by Mary Jo Salter. Used by permission of Alfred A. Knopf, an imprint of the Knopf Doubleday Publishing Group, a division of Penguin Random House LLC. All rights reserved.

"The Baseball Players" from White Apples and the Taste of Stone by Donald Hall. Copyright © 2006 by Donald Hall. Used by permission of HarperCollins Publishers.

"Sunday in the Old Republic" from THE ARKANSAS TESTAMENT by Derek Walcott. Copyright © 1987 by Derek Walcott. Reprinted by permission of Farrar, Straus and Giroux. All Rights Reserved.

"Powers of Congress". Copyright © 199 by Alice Fulton, from POWERS OF CONGRESS by Alice Fulton. Used by permission of W. W. Norton & Company, Inc.

"Used", first published in Atlantic Monthly, July 1989. © by Rita Dove. Reprinted by permission of the author.

"Among Children," copyright © 1992 by Philip Levine; from WHAT WORK IS by Philip Levine. Used by permission of Alfred A. Knopf, an imprint of the Knopf Doubleday Publishing Group, a division of Penguin Random House LLC. All rights reserved.

"Darling" By permission of the author, Naomi Shihab Nye, 2024.

"Benediction" from THE STUDY OF HUMAN LIFE by Joshua Bennett, copyright © 2022 by Joshua Bennett. Used by permission of Penguin Books, an imprint of Penguin Publishing Group, a division of Penguin Random House LLC. All rights reserved.

This poem from "Foretaste" by Margaret Pont appears courtesy of Sunstone Press.
"Northeast Coast" Reprinted by permission of Joan Blackburn.

"July Mountain" from OPUS POSTHUMOUS by Wallace Stevens, copyright © 1957 by Elsie Stevens and Holly Stevens. Used by permission of Alfred A. Knopf, an imprint of the Knopf Doubleday Publishing Group, a division of Penguin Random House LLC. All rights reserved.

"A Winter Ship" from THE COLOSSUS by Sylvia Plath, copyright © 1957, 1958, 1959, 1960, 1961, 1962 by Sylvia Plath. Used by permission of Alfred A. Knopf, an imprint of the Knopf Doubleday Publishing Group, a division of Penguin Random House LLC. All rights reserved.

"A Winter Ship" from by Sylvia Plath. Used in Canada with permission from Faber and Faber Ltd.

"Fighting for Roses" Copyright © Estate of Muriel Rukeyser, 2005 Reprinted by permission of Estate of Muriel Rukeyser.

Maxine Kumin, “January 25th.” Used by the permission of the Maxine Kumin Literary Trust.

“The Last Wolverine” from The Whole Motion: Collected Poems 1945-1992 © 1992 by James Dickey. Published by Wesleyan University Press. Used by permission.

“Early December in Croton-on-Hudson” from The First Four Books of Poems by Louise Gluck. Copyright ©1968, 1971, 1972, 1973, 1974, 1975, 1976, 1977, 1978, 1979, 1980, 1985, 1995 by Louise Glück. Used by permission of HarperCollins Publishers.

Charles Wright “April,” Country Music: Selected Early Poems © 1991 Charles Wright. Published by Wesleyan University Press and used by permission.

“On the Disadvantages of Central Heating” from THE COLLECTED POEMS OF AMY CLAMPITT by Amy Clampitt, copyright © 1997 by the Estate of Amy Clampitt. Used by permission of Alfred A. Knopf, an imprint of the Knopf Doubleday Publishing Group, a division of Penguin Random House LLC. All rights reserved.

”Night-Blooming Cereus” copyright Katha Politt.

“Chord” from THE RAIN IN THE TREES by W. S. Merwin, copyright © 1988 by W. S. Merwin. Used by permission of Alfred A. Knopf, an imprint of the Knopf Doubleday Publishing Group, a division of Penguin Random House LLC. All rights reserved.

Linda Gregg, “Last Night in Mithymna” from All of It Singing: New and Selected Poems. Copyright © 1992 by Linda Gregg. Reprinted with the permission of The Permissions Company, LLC on behalf of Graywolf Press, graywolfpress.org.

“In Answer to Amy's Question ‘What's a Pickerel?’” from The Marriage in the Trees by Stanley Plumly. Copyright (c) 1997 by Stanley Plumly. Used by permission of HarperCollins Publishers.

“Song”. Copyright © 1991 by Rosanna Warren, from STAINED GLASS by Rosanna Warren. Used by permission of W. W. Norton & Company, Inc.

“What I Did on A Rainy Day” © May Swenson. Used with permission of The Literary Estate of May Swenson. All rights reserved.

“Mockingbirds” from White Pine by Mary Oliver. Copyright © 1994, 1993, 1992, 1991 by Mary Oliver. Used by permission of HarperCollins Publishers.

“Dooryard Flower” from SHADOW OF HEAVEN by Ellen Bryant Voigt. Copyright © 2002 by Ellen Bryant Voigt. Used by permission of W. W. Norton & Company, Inc.

"Come In" by Robert Frost from THE POETRY OF ROBERT FROST edited by Edward Connery Lathem. Copyright © 1969 by Henry Holt and Company. Copyright © 1936 by Robert Frost, copyright © 1964 by Lesley Frost Ballantine. Reprinted by permission of Henry Holt and Company. All Rights Reserved.

William Stafford, "Circle of Breath" from Ask Me: 100 Essential Poems. Originally in The Atlantic (1954). Copyright 1954, © 2014 by William Stafford and the Estate of William Stafford. Reprinted with the permission of The Permissions Company, LLC on behalf of Graywolf Press, Minneapolis, Minnesota, graywolfpress.org.

"Eleutheria" from COLLECTED POEMS © 1971 by James Wright. Published by Wesleyan University Press. Used by permission.

AK Ramanujan, "Anxiety." Used by the permission of the estate of A.K. Ramanujan.

"The Lost Pilot" by James Tate. Copyright © 1966 by James Tate. Reprinted by permission of Georges Borchardt, Inc., for the Estate of James Tate.

"Last Words" from COLLECTED POEMS by James Merrill, edited by J. D. McClatchy and Stephen Yenser, copyright © 2001 by the Literary Estate of James Merrill at Washington University. Used by permission of Alfred A. Knopf, an imprint of the Knopf Doubleday Publishing Group, a division of Penguin Random House LLC. All rights reserved.

Margaret Atwood, "Girl and Horse, 1928" Copyright © O.W.Toad Lt, 1970 Reprinted by permission of CAA on behalf of O.W. Toad Ltd.

"The Ghosts", first published in Atlantic Monthly, July 1973, by the poet formally known as Kathryn Ungerer.

"The Name of the Air" Permission of the Estate of Phillip Levine.

"Heroic Simile" from Praise by Robert Hass. Copyright © 1979 by Robert Hass. Used by permission of HarperCollins Publishers.

"Monarchs" from Satan Says, by Sharon Olds, © 1980. Reprinted by permission of the University of Pittsburgh Press.

Tess Gallagher, "Sudden Journey" from Midnight Lantern: New and Selected Poems. Copyright © 2006 by Tess Gallagher. Reprinted with the permission of The Permissions Company, LLC on behalf of Graywolf Press, graywolfpress.org.

"A Visitor" from DREAM WORK by Mary Oliver, copyright © 1986 by NW Orchard LLC. Used by permission of Penguin Books, an imprint of Penguin Publishing Group, a division of Penguin Random House LLC. All rights reserved. Reprinted by the permission of The Charlotte Sheedy Literary Agency as agent for the author. Copyright © 1986 by Mary Oliver with permission of Bill Reichblum.

"The Wide and Varied World", from THE LOTUS FLOWERS by Ellen Bryant Voigt. Copyright © 1987 by Ellen Bryant Voigt. Used by permission of W. W. Norton & Company, Inc.

"Execution" from THE NIGHT PARADE by Edward Hirsch, copyright © 1989 by Edward Hirsch. Used by permission of Alfred A. Knopf, an imprint of the Knopf Doubleday Publishing Group, a division of Penguin Random House LLC. All rights reserved.

"Late Loving" from NEAR CHANGES by Mona Van Duyn, copyright © 1990 by Mona Van Duyn. Used by permission of Alfred A. Knopf, an imprint of the Knopf Doubleday Publishing Group, a division of Penguin Random House LLC. All rights reserved.

"The Bad Physician" Linda Gregerson, The Woman Who Dies in Her Sleep, New York: Houghton Mifflin, 1996.

"What the Living Do", from WHAT THE LIVING DO by Marie Howe. Copyright © 1997 by Marie Howe. Used by permission of W. W. Norton & Company, Inc.

Carl Phillips, "As from a Quiver of Arrows" from From the Devotions. Originally from The Atlantic (October 1995). Copyright © 1995, 2002 by Carl Phillips. Reprinted with the permission of The Permissions Company, LLC on behalf of Graywolf Press, Minneapolis, Minnesota, graywolfpress.org.

"Colostrum" from BOOK OF HOURS: POEMS by Kevin Young, copyright © 2014 by Kevin Young. Used by permission of Alfred A. Knopf, an imprint of the Knopf Doubleday Publishing Group, a division of Penguin Random House LLC. All rights reserved.

"Ars Poetica with Mother and Dogs" from GOLDEN AX by Rio Cortez, copyright © 2022 by Rio Cortez. Used by permission of Penguin Books, an imprint of Penguin Publishing Group, a division of Penguin Random House LLC. All rights reserved.

ACKNOWLEDGMENTS

This book has had a tremendous amount of support from colleagues, family, and friends. Special thanks to the students in the Poetic Research Group—Jake Bridge, Molly McLaughlin, Susie Kim, Anna Oestreich, and Ryan Pfeiffer—for reading the entire manuscript multiple times. Student collaboration was made possible through an Experimental Humanities faculty grant. Thanks to David Gerdes, Joy Ward, Eric Kaler, and my colleagues in the College of Arts and Sciences at Case Western Reserve University.

Working with writers and editors at *The Atlantic* has been one of the most important intellectual gifts of my life. I thank Ann Hulbert for her reminders that the given shape of things holds infinite possibilities. Peter Mendelsund and Paul Spella came up with a beautiful design and cover. Thanks to Katherine Hu, Allison Prevatt, Janice Wolly, and Sarah Yager for their help with fact-checks, copyright clearance, and editing—and for their perpetual good humor as we turned over various poetic stones that had been at rest for decades. Faith Hill's vigorous and transformative editing of poetry helped to create the roster of poets in this book. Thanks to Adrienne LaFrance and John Swansburg for cheerfully enduring screenshots of poems in the small hours of the morning. Thanks to Jeffrey Goldberg for our conversations about the echoes of poetry and fiction across time.

I'm especially grateful for the work of two careful, thoughtful editors at Zando: Sarah Goldstein and Sarah Ried. Molly Stern's enthusiasm for the project has been invaluable from the start. Thanks to the copyeditors and production team at the press for their hard work in assembling a book that comprises almost two centuries of poetry.

Lindsay Turner and I met twenty years ago over a poem we'd both memorized. I hope this anthology falls into the hands of young readers who can discover the changing music of poetry in its pages. I have in mind Madeleine Carey Rock, who will find much to savor here, and Julian Henry Turner Hunter, to whom the book is dedicated.

ABOUT THE AUTHORS

WALT HUNTER is senior associate dean of the College of Arts and Sciences and professor of English at Case Western Reserve University. He is the author of two books of criticism, *Forms of a World: Contemporary Poetry and the Making of Globalization* (2019) and *The American House Poem, 1945–2021* (2023), and a book of poetry, *Some Flowers* (2022). He is the poetry and fiction editor of *The Atlantic*.

DR. JOSHUA BENNETT is the Distinguished Chair of the Humanities and professor of literature at MIT. He is the author of five books, including *Spoken Word: A Cultural History* (Knopf, 2023), which was named a *New York Times* Notable Book and a Best Book of the Year by *The New Yorker*; *The Study of Human Life* (Penguin, 2022), which won the Paterson Poetry Prize and was adapted for television in collaboration with Warner Brothers Studios, and *The Sobbing School* (Penguin, 2016), winner of the National Poetry Series and a finalist for an NAACP Image Award.

Bennett earned his PhD in English from Princeton University, and an MA in theatre and performance studies from the University of Warwick, where he was a Marshall Scholar. He has recited his original works at the Sundance Film Festival, the NAACP Image Awards, and President Obama's Evening of Poetry and Music at the White House. He has also performed and taught creative writing workshops at hundreds of middle schools, high schools, colleges, and universities across the United States, as well as in the UK and South Africa.

For his creative writing and scholarship, Bennett has received fellowships and awards from the Guggenheim Foundation, the Whiting Foundation, the Institute for Advanced Study, the National Endowment for the Arts, and the Society of Fellows at Harvard University. He lives in Massachusetts with his family.